THE BALLOON BUSINESS KIT

The Balloon Business Kit

By Margie Padgitt

First Edition

ISBN: 978-0-9988558-2-0

Publisher: HearthMasters Publishing
div of HearthMasters, Inc.

To contact the publisher by mail, write to:
HearthMasters Publishing
PO Box 1166
Independence, MO 64051

Contact the author: margepadgitt@comcast.net

Printed in the United States of America

Cover art and some interior art: Clipart.com

Dedicated to all of the hard-working professional balloon
decorating artists and entertainers in the world

Table of Contents

Introduction

I've been fortunate to have owned a number of different types of businesses. Some of these failed, some I just grew tired of, but most have been and are successful. I have the perspective of a veteran business owner and the reader can learn from my experiences.

Prior to taking the leap to owing my own company I started out working for my father at the age of 12. He was a successful salesman for Encyclopaedia Britannica and showed me the ropes of selling. I was his office assistant and went on sales calls with him. Later I worked for a number of businesses then studied business and communication at CMSU, UMC and UMKC.

I opened and operated a floral shop and cake decorating business for 11 years before adding balloons and changing the name to Balloon Events. This became a corporate balloon decorating company serving the greater Kansas City area. We ran that operation for an additional 10 years. The only reason I closed the balloon company was due to health issues that I had, as well as one of my key employees. We both have Fibromyalgia, which prevented us from working long hours or standing for any length of time. Prior to that my husband and I opened a chimney contracting company in 1982, and still operate it today. We have 16 employees and are the largest business of its type in the Midwest region. I also own a publishing company and publish my own books, other's books, and two magazines. And as if that weren't enough to keep us busy, my husband and I started a real estate investment company in 2015 and it was turning a profit within six months.

I've learned a thing or two about what works and what doesn't work in business.

Whether you are new to the balloon industry or a seasoned veteran, this kit will assist you in the unique balloon business. Included in this book are most of the things you need to know about running a successful balloon décor, retail, or entertainer business.

I sincerely hope that this publication will assist you in getting a good start, or if you are already established, an even greater bottom line. Good Luck in your endeavors!

Sincerely,

Margie Padgitt

Getting Started in the Balloon Business

If you ask anyone in business if they had enough working capital to start with they would say no. This is because each of them underestimated the costs to run a business. Some of these entrepreneurs were able to overcome the lack of adequate funding, higher expenses than anticipated and succeed anyway, but most do not. In fact, the chances of any business getting to the five year mark are slim.

But you can minimize your risk by planning in advance, creating a business plan, and *knowing* what you are getting into, rather than guessing. This section applies to you even if you're already in business.

Business plan information is available at bookstores and online. I suggest you get a book about how to write a business plan or get one through SCORE. Start by listing your anticipated expenses including supplies, equipment, office furniture, computers, vehicles, marketing, labor, rent, etc.

Start with working capital that will get you through at least 12 months without expecting a profit. This means figuring out how much money it will take to run your business through 12 months and obtaining that amount of working capital through a bank loan, personal loans from friends or family, or your own money you've set aside for this purpose.

Getting a bank loan for a start-up business is very difficult these days. The bank will expect to see your business plan, your qualified staff resume's, your location, and will want to know how much of your own money you are putting at risk. They usually expect you to invest at least 25% of the total amount needed. You will likely need to offer collateral to secure the loan, so have a list of items ready and their value included. These items should be paid off and free and clear. You can use a Certificate of Deposit, bonds, your house, or perhaps a late model vehicle. You may have better luck at a small bank rather than a large bank due to the bad loan hits recently, their loan guidelines are now much stricter.

After obtaining your working capital, put it in the bank and leave it there for business expenses only. Do not dip into the till for personal expenses or whims. Keep it all business and you will have a higher likelihood of success.

Resist the temptation to start additional businesses until this one is well established and running on its own without your immediate supervision.

Successful entrepreneurs put good people in place to run the business for them, so the operation can operate on its own after a period of time (usually 3-5 years). So plan to get all of your employees highly trained.

If you are already established you may want to skip this section, or review it to be sure you have everything covered.

Step 1: Obtain a Federal EIN
Step 2: Register with the State
Step 3: Get a DUNS number
Step 4: Obtain Insurance
Step 5: Design a Logo
Step 6: Get Business Training
Step 7: Get Capital
Step 8: Obtain Equipment and Supplies
Step 9: Open for Business

Step 1: Obtain an EIN

An Employer Identification Number (EIN) is also known as a Federal Tax Identification Number, and is used to identify a business entity. All, businesses need an EIN before starting operations. You may apply for an EIN directly from the IRS website at https://www.irs.gov/Businesses/Small-Businesses-&-Self-Employed/Employer-ID-Numbers-EINs.

This is a free service offered by the Internal Revenue Service and you can get your EIN immediately. You must check with your state to make sure you need a state number or charter.

Step 2: Register with the State

1. Decide on a name and apply for a fictitious name registration at your state's Secretary of State webpage to save the name and make sure that no one else is using it. You may do a search for names on the website first. If you should decide to operate as a sole proprietor, you may then use this name for your business.

2. After you have decided what the legal structure of your company will be (see below), register as a new business online at the Secretary of State's website.

3. Register with your state Department of Revenue to obtain a Tax ID number to use when filing your state tax returns. Also get a Retail sales tax and/or Use tax number, which you will need in order to purchase supplies at wholesale. If you do not have a retail store, you may just want to get a Use tax number and set up as a service business. This will save you the hassle of collecting retail sales tax and submitting it to the state. The office should have a booklet which will assist you in getting everything you need to start doing business. Do not start doing business until you have these items completed.

keep a substantial amount of profits in your LLC.

S Corporations, or "Subchapter S" corporations, produce several benefits as compared to sole proprietorships, partnerships, and C corporations. The biggest benefits are eliminating your personal liability and liability for debts, and payroll tax savings. There is no self-employment tax, so the average business making $90,000 per year will save $7,000 in taxes. Tax accounting is easier with an S Corporation than a Partnership.

Other benefits are that losses can be used as tax deductions on the shareholders personal income tax return, and that the corporation isn't taxed on the corporation profits. Profits and losses flow through to the shareholders and are included in their personal income taxes. An S corporation does not pay Corporate Income Tax like a C corporation does.

The main downsides to incorporating is that the tax preparation is more difficult, and you'll likely need a professional to do it; and you'll have more expense for legal, accounting, and bookkeeping services.

C Corporations are reserved for large companies with multiple shareholders. The accounting and recordkeeping requirements are the most stringent and time consuming. I do not recommend this type of entity for a small business with fewer than 100 employees.

My company is an S corporation and I also own two LLC's. Either of these would be most appropriate and offer the most security for a balloon décor or entertaining business. For more information on business entities visit your Secretary of State's Website or Legal Zoom.com or I suggest the book *Incorporating Your Business for Dummies* by Carl R. J. Sniffen.

Your Business Ownership

If you are a minority or woman-owned business, you have some advantages over other companies. It may not be fair, but that is the way it is right now. The biggest advantage is obtaining large government or private sector jobs since most agencies must set aside a certain percentage of work for WBE (Woman-owned Business Enterprise) or MBE (Minority-owned) Business Enterprises. If your company is 51% or more woman or minority owned, it may qualify.

If you have not set up your business as an LLC or S Corporation yet, and you are a minority or woman, you may want to consider putting at least 51% of the business in your name. However, in getting to know other companies who do a lot of work for large contractors I've found that it is easier to get approved through the SBA if it is 100% owned by a woman or minority. The 51% owner must be an ACTIVE owner in the business doing daily activity and making as much money or more than the other owners or employees.

In order to get an official listing as a WBE or MBE you will need to apply through the Small Business Administration at www.sba.gov or for women you may also go to http://www.nwboc.org/section_apply.

There is a lot of paperwork and the process takes months to get through, but is worth it if you want to do large contracts.

Step 3: Get a DUNS Number

If you want to do business with larger clients or city, county, state, or Federal Government, or larger corporations you'll need to get a D-U-N-S Number, which is the industry standard for business listings. You may already have a DUNS number assigned, or you many need to establish a new profile. The D&B D-U-N-S Number has become the standard for keeping track of the world's businesses.

If a supplier is planning on doing business with you they will usually check your DUNS credit rating. This is your *business* credit rating, not your *personal* credit rating. DUNS is recognized, recommended and/or required by more than 50 global, industry and trade associations, including the United Nations and the U.S. Federal Government.

Go to www.smallbusiness.dnb.com to register your business

There is no charge to register. When you apply you'll receive a unique nine-digit identifier for a single business entity, that also links corporate families together. If you'd like to keep track of who is checking on your company or changes in your credit profile, you will need to become a member and pay for the service. After you apply the first time, a D&B sales person will contact you to try to sell you this service. Realize that it is not necessary to pay for membership, but if you think you need to keep track of your credit rating and keep your business information current, it may be a good idea to do this. It is a good idea to check your profile periodically to make sure that everything is current. Be sure to add as much information as possible to your credit profile such as profit and loss statements, annual income, number of employees, etc. and update this periodically. Be aware that there could be incorrect information or missing information on your report that you will need to correct.

D&B has other services as well including new business tips, web design services, online marketing, sales leads and marketing lists, and checking other businesses reports. Visit the website to get all of the details.

Establish Business Credit

Now that you have a DUNS number, open a bank account in your business name, then get a business debit card. I suggest using a local community credit union because their fees are very low and some even give back money at the end of the year since they are non-profits. Some credit unions don't do business with S Corporations.

Next, apply for a business only credit card from any major credit card bank. I suggest Capital One (www.capitalone.com) because there are some perks you can choose from including airline miles, cash refunds, or gift purchases with points. Look for a 0% interest rate card, usually offered for the first year. Buy all of your equipment and supplies, and gas using this card in order to get as many points or airline miles as possible. I know one family of four who travels to Hawaii every year for free just because they use their card for purchases.

Always pay on time, and pay in full every month so you do not incur interest charges, which can be very high. You can set up automatic payments drafted from your bank account.

Step 4: Get Insurance

Insurance is a requirement for anyone doing business. Make sure you have adequate insurance before doing one job or hiring one employee. Some of your larger clients may request a certificate of insurance prior to doing business with you. Here are some guidelines for the company doing balloon décor or entertainment work:

Liability Insurance

Liability insurance covers you and your company if something you or your employees do causes an injury to a person or damage to someone else's property. Although it might be hard to think of anything you could possibly do to cause harm in the balloon business, there is the real risk of an accident. Helium tanks fall, children put balloons in their mouths, and large balloons pop in people's faces. No matter how careful you are, an accident could happen.

A minimum of $500,000 in liability insurance coverage is what I suggest for all businesses. You may want to have more coverage if you do corporate work. This insurance is relatively inexpensive but is usually paid for by the year or by the month. The rate is based on your exposure, and most insurance companies base that rate on your payroll and annual gross income. Many insurance companies provide this type of business insurance. You may want to go to a broker to find insurance since he/she will have more insurance companies to choose from.

Worker's Compensation

All states have different requirements, so you may want to call your state board to find out when Worker's Comp is required. Some state laws require no insurance for a sole proprietor who has no employees, but insurance is necessary when you hire one or more employees. The owner may not be required to have Worker's Compensation on him/herself.

For a corporation, usually all employees (including the owner) are required to have it. Rate is based on the type of work you do and total payroll. Audits are done annually, and you will be required to file a report quarterly or monthly. Note: I have found that it is very difficult to get Workmen's Comp to pay for an owner's injury. You are usually better off with regular health insurance, although if you do have workmen's comp you cannot use the health insurance for a work-related injury. I HIGHLY suggest getting this insurance for all of you employees! By having it, your employees cannot sue you or your business for any work injury.

Most standard insurance agents do NOT handle Worker's Comp, so you will need to find a business insurance broker who can find one for you. Worker's comp insurance covers accidental injury and accidental death while working on the job or traveling to or from the job. I hope you never need to use it, but the fact is that accidents do happen.

In some states, Worker's Compensation Insurance is not required if you are a sole proprietor and have no employees. However, it is a good idea to have this insurance anyway. Some people won't allow you on their property if you don't have WC, and most larger contractors you may sub for or government purchasers will require it. We carry two million but you may need a different amount. Your agent should be able to help with determining what you need, or you may be required to carry a certain amount by your clients.

Worker's comp rates are determined by the state and by type of work you do by Class Codes. Look up the class codes and rates in your state and try to use the code that best describes what you do but is the least expensive. Watch your insurance company or auditor each year as they may try to move your workers in to a higher class code rating. For instance sales is different than entertainer, but if you do any entertaining work at all the company may try to put your entire salary in that classification.

A way to get around this is to keep track of the type of work and divide your work in to percentages if your state will allow this. Google "worker's comp codes" and your state name. Rates are determined annually and revised every three years in my state. So a claim will stay on the books for three to four years and affect your rates. For minor injuries, take care of it yourself. But for major injuries on the job, you'll need to turn it in. If there is a claim, you will have a MOD (modification) rating by the insurance company. This rating will affect your rates for at least three years, so you don't want that to happen!

An audit will be completed annually either in person or with forms you need to fill out and send in. Rates are also based on your gross income and employee work hours and salaries. Audits determine whether you paid too little or too much the previous year and an adjustment will be made to your account accordingly. The payments you've already made for the previous year were an ESTIMATE only and were not based on actual payroll.

Worker's Comp has a few rules to follow in order to get the best rates. You'll probably be required to have a Safety Coordinator assigned, a Safety Policy (written), regular safety meetings, and the company will assign a certain medical facility for you and your employees to go to in case of an injury. You can usually save about 10% by following the company's procedures. Ask a commercial insurance broker for more information and rates.

Realize that Worker's Comp only pays a portion of the salary for the employee's time off of work, and medical bills. The employee may want to get an attorney to get the best settlement. WC does not cover loss of income for the company due to the employee being off of work, time spent by office staff for the reports and contact with Doctors and insurance. And you can't take away the employee's pain or the family's loss in the case of a death.

You may want to inform the homeowner that if they hire someone who does not have Worker's Comp they will be liable for any injuries the worker may sustain while on their property.

It is best to be OVERLY CAUTIOUS and take precautions and follow OSHA guidelines to AVOID ACCIDENTS so they don't happen in the first place.

Equipment Insurance

Insure your equipment when it would be a hardship if you were without it. It is very easy to acquire a lot of expensive equipment in the balloon business, and the insurance is usually affordable (although the prices have been going up lately). Make sure to insure your office furniture, computers, printers, fax machine, etc, too. If you work out of your home, your homeowner's policy most likely will NOT cover anything used in your business! Most business insurance companies handle this type of insurance.

Auto Insurance

Everyone has liability insurance, theft, and collision coverages with their auto insurance, but make sure that the medical payment provision is enough on your policy. Many policies only allow for only $5,000 in medical payments, which is extremely low. You may want to make it at least $50,000 per person or more in medical coverage. You could be sued personally, or your corporation could be sued if you were found liable in an accident, and you could potentially lose everything.

Make sure that all of your employees names are on your business auto insurance or they may not be covered!
Note: Assure that any employee listed as a driver has a good driving record or your rates could go up. We insist that if an employee gets a ticket either on or off the job, they hire an attorney to get the ticket reduced to a non-moving violation.

Homeowner/Building Insurance

If you work from home it is a good idea to review your homeowner's policy to see if there is coverage for any business furniture, office supplies, equipment, or inventory, or liability for accidents on your property. It likely does not, so you may want to obtain a new policy to cover your home since it is being used for business.

If you have a warehouse, office, or retail space, you'll need to insure the property and contents with a business broker.

The Certificate of Insurance

Provide a certificate of insurance to any client who asks for it. This is just proof to your client that you carry the proper insurance and makes them feel more comfortable. Your corporate clients will probably be the only ones who request this. Just call your broker and ask them to fax you a copy and send the client a copy with the clients name and address as the named insured. Then keep your copy in the client's file.

Health Insurance

Health Insurance is mandatory for any company who wants to retain good employees. Group rates usually start at five employees or more. If you are married and your spouse works in the company, you can get the insurance set up with his/her own policy instead of adding them as a spouse, which costs the same, but you get the added employee count if you need it. Each state has different rules regarding group health insurance, so you'll want to check with a broker who can help you with this.

I suggest using a business insurance broker who can put together a package for all of your insurance needs. Most companies offer a discount if you have two or more types of insurance with them. For instance, we have our auto and liability with one company and receive a discount for doing so. To find a business insurance broker, just to a search on the internet or ask your friends in business who they would recommend.

When NOT to file an insurance claim:

Insurance is meant for catastrophic events. Only file a claim when you really need to, because each time a claim is filed it is a strike against you. You will be considered to be a higher risk and your premiums may go up. Some experts recommend only filing a claim over $3,000, and

anything under that you pay for yourself. This is called "self-insurance."

☞ **Tips**

To keep insurance costs down

- Only file a claim for larger amounts and cover the small costs yourself

- Get all of your insurance with one company to get a multi-line discount

- Raise your deductible to $1,000 or more

- Install an anti-theft alarm system on your office and vehicles

- I nstall smoke detectors and fire extinguishers
  - Install dead bolts on doors

- Make sure you have a Safety Policy , including regular training in place for Worker's Comp discounts

- Get quotes annually from two or three brokers

Marketing Your Business

Marketing and PR are critical to the success of your business. Marketing is promotion using print, radio, T.V. or other methods and is commonly thought of as advertising, although it is much more than that. PR or "Public Relations", is promoting the good will of your company and keeping your name out in the public eye, without blatant advertising. Both are good for business, and the savvy business owner will utilize any and all methods at his/her disposal.

I found that when I first started out in business in the early 1980's that the Yellow Pages was the best form of advertising and brought us the most clients. After we were in business for a few years I noticed that our best customers (and repeat customers) came from referrals. And since the internet has gained in popularity with over 3/4 of all American households now using it, our website is now the best bang for the buck. Different types of advertising need to be implemented by any type of business in order to be successful.

Keep in mind that business owners must be aware of changes in consumer buying habits and watch results from all forms of advertising carefully. My assistant has a check box on our inquiry form that s indicates how the person found out about our company, and she just has to check off which one it is. Sometimes the result is two items and the second item is our website. The customer will say "I heard about you from so-and-so then checked out your website. If it is a referral, she writes the person's name on the form so that we can send them a thank you or a gift for their consideration. This small gesture will go a long way and keep the referrals coming.

Balloon businesses, whether decorators or entertainers, are unique and require some inventive ideas to market their company. After all, that is what is expected by the public, who is usually looking for some form of entertainment or "Wow" factor to brighten their event when they call you. Since this is hardly a mainstream business, you'll be thinking outside the square box quite often. Since most balloon company owners are very inventive I'm sure you'll come up with ideas to add to my list.

Marketing outside the norm takes a little extra time and effort, but the results can be well worth it. The things you do to market your business are extremely important, not only for the "bottom line," but for the image that you want to project to your potential and current clients. In order to compete with other businesses or just to maintain your current customer base, your business must always appear to be up to date on the latest techniques and ideas, have good customer service, and do something that other companies in your industry don't. Of course, you do these things anyway, but to convey these ideas to the public you need a marketing plan. For businesses that don't have a marketing plan, I can assure you that their business will stagnate and eventually die.

Avoiding traps: As a business owner, you get bombarded on a daily basis with people trying to sell you advertising. Some sales people will even go as far as to make you feel obligated to purchase advertising from them by offering you a pre written "article" for their newspaper, a pre-made website, or other item, which shows how much work they have already done for free for you. Don't fall in to that trap. Whatever they made up for you will not be as good as if you hired a pro or did it yourself. You know your business best – so I suggest writing your own ads or putting what you want conveyed on paper and turning it over to a professional. The results will always be better.

About print advertising: Unless you own a car dealership or huge furniture store and have unlimited funds to spend on print ads, don't waste your money on large ad contracts with newspapers or coupon books. The percentage of calls that result are too low for the small business person to reap benefits from the ad. Instead, I suggest starting out with very small ads and running them on a weekly basis. Plan on keeping your ad in for at least six months, because print advertising usually does not yield results right away. My suggestion is to stay away from print advertising during the first few years of business due to the expense.

Free Advertising: Free advertising is always the best type of advertising. Any time you can get an article printed in a newspaper or newsletter, people read it as news rather than an ad. Many people read the entire paper from front to back, and most ads are ignored unless the reader is looking for something in particular. An article written by you or about you is considered by the reader to be *news* instead of *advertising*. This can make you appear to be an expert, which you are, on your topic. Take this opportunity to give the consumer information that is helpful, and don't do a hard sell on your products or services. Getting an article about your business printed in a newspaper is not easy, but it can be done.

The best method to get attention is to send a press release (*see section on press releases*) about a newsworthy event. I've had news stories printed and on TV simply because I knew someone at the newspaper or TV station and contacted them about a story. I met these people through networking at a chamber of commerce meeting. If an event is truly newsworthy and you don't bother people with frequently, you'll find that they'll be willing to talk with you about it. Ultimately, it is the program producer or editor who decides what story gets printed or aired. Smaller newspapers and TV stations are usually more likely to accept your story that large media companies.

Yellow Pages: Print advertising is out—most people look online for what they want using their smart phones or computer. There is a YP website, but anyone can find the same thing using Google or other search engine. However, if you live in a smaller community you may want to use the print Yellow Pages.

Your logo: Always use your logo on every piece of advertising to "brand" your business. Put your logo on your business cards, in the yellow pages, brochures,--everything! And if you don't have a logo, hire a professional graphics artist to make one for you.

Networking: Networking is probably the most important thing you can do to market your business. People like to do business with people they know because they feel they can trust them. It is worth the extra effort to cultivate relationships with other business owners because they will become your best clients. Business owners love to refer business to others, because they know they will get referrals in return. Many associations and networking groups also offer educational opportunities at meetings, so this is a bonus and may be a real help in getting ideas for running your business.

Some examples of networking groups are the Chamber of Commerce, American Business Women's Association, and the Convention and Visitor's Bureau. Some are associations, others are just for networking for business owners only such as a breakfast club. Some charge a fee – others are free to join. There are many others – look in the yellow pages and on the internet to find groups near you.

Not all networking groups are going to work. I suggest trying one out for a few months, and if it looks like it is not working for you, leave and find a different association or group that will better suit your needs. A warning about expensive "exclusive" networking groups – I suggest not wasting your money on them. Some charge hundreds of dollars to belong to an exclusive club that has only 20 or so people at meetings. If you don't have a product or service that everyone will need soon, the high expense does not warrant the few sales that result.

Trucks and Vans: Vehicles do much more than transport you to and from the job site and to get supplies and materials. They are moving billboard advertisements of your business. Use them to your advantage, and take the tax write-off, too. Any type of signage is better than no sign, but the bigger the better. And don't ever go to a job "incognito" where there is no sign on your vehicle at all. It is just not professional, and it says "I can't afford a sign, so I am not successful." People want the people they do business with to be successful because it gives them confidence that you know what you are doing.

Signs should be proportionate to the vehicle, stand out so they get noticed, and look professional. An easy and inexpensive way to get a professional look is to go to a vinyl sign company (hey, that networking paid off!) and ask them for advice on how to letter your truck. You can just do lettering or add graphics (your logo) and a photo of what you do. It is my opinion that a color photo of your work (or a wrap) is the best advertising you can do on a vehicle. People will get the point when they see your truck or van if they need your service, you may get a call immediately after they see it. And customers will know it is you when you pull up in their driveway. This is especially important to women. They want to know that the person standing on their step is the person they called and not someone *pretending* to be the person you called. Remember that the vehicle should also always be CLEAN so it looks neat and your sign can be read easily.

You may want to use the work vehicle even when not working, such as for trips to the grocery store or going out to eat. The reason is obvious – advertising. My husband took one of our box

trucks used in our chimney business to the grocery store one evening and after he was in the store a few minutes, he heard over the loudspeaker *"will the person with the chimney van please come to the front counter?"* Twice. He thought something happened to the truck and envisioned it going out of gear and rolling down the parking lot into oncoming traffic. My husband RAN to the front counter. The store owner just wanted his card so he could get his chimney relined.

Employee Appearance: I can't stress enough how important it is to your customer to see a clean, neatly groomed and dressed service person working in their home or business. This is a huge statement – it says "I care about being neat and clean, so I'll take good care of your home or venue."

Make sure that your logo and company name is embroidered on the shirts. This is another id for your client. It also looks professional and is good advertising when employees go to the store to pick up supplies or go to lunch. You can get this service from a local embroidery shop. Hats are another item to embroider and give a finished look to the uniform.

As for dress to networking events, don't go right after working all day in a dirty uniform. Go home and change into business attire, and perhaps a button-down shirt embroidered with your logo or a suit jacket (for men and women) with a name tag pinned to it. Nice looking name tags can be purchased at Office Max or from a printer. You want to look like the successful business owner, not an employee.

Barter Clubs: Barter clubs are becoming very popular among business owners. They have been around for a long time – the oldest club was

started in 1960 and now has over 60,000 members plus another 100,00 "trade partners" worldwide. I highly suggest joining at least one of these barter networking groups to increase sales.

Here's how barter clubs work: Member businesses buy and sell from each other using "barter dollars." The barter dollars are kept in a barter bank by the administrating organization, and are available for the member to use anytime with any other member of the group to make purchases of goods and services. All members must own a business that can be utilized by the other members in the club. A fee is assessed by the club, usually part barter and part cash. Most barter clubs issue a monthly statement so you can keep track of your sales, purchases, and fees. The fees are 100% tax deductible. The advantage to joining a barter club is that you don't have to worry about trying to find someone to do a direct trade with, and then collecting their part of the bargain from them after you have provided a service. I have been burned more than once by people I did direct trades with and it is not a good experience. There is safety in the barter club. Another advantage is that you have a whole new set of possible customers who are waiting to do business with you! Check out **www.itex.com** to see the one of the barter clubs I belong to and really enjoy doing business through. Do mention my name when you call! Their number is 918-298-2266

The Internet

Email: Having an e-mail address is a must for any business owner today. We do half of our business communication in this manner. Many clients contact us through our website initially, and I usually send proposals to them via e-mail by attaching a PDF file. You can get a free PDF filemaker at www.software112.com which converts your word processing program file such as Word or Publisher into a PDF file so the person receiving it can open it. Not everyone has the same programs, but everyone has or can get the free acrobat reader, which is required to open PDF files. Go to www.acrobat.com if you don't already have the reader on your computer. Adobe also has software to make, edit, and convert PDF files.

Signature line: A good marketing technique I've been using for years is to place a signature line at the bottom of every e-mail you send out. This should include your name, business name, address, phone, fax, website, and e-mail address. You'd be surprised how much business can come your way when you do this. Just set you e-mail program to include your signature automatically.

Advertise on the Internet: The first place I recommend is Google at www.google.com—type in "adwords" and read all about how you can advertise when anyone in your area types in a key word like "balloon." The second place I recommend advertising is a Yahoo Local. After you have set these up, consider exchanging links with other websites such as wedding planners, event sites, etc. You'll have to do some searching on the internet in order to find local businesses who are willing to exchange links.

Social Media:
Social medial sites like Facebook are commonly used to share and communicate among all age groups. Be sure to make a page for your business as well as your personal page in order to keep your business in front of the public. Ads may be purchased to boost your image to more people. Be sure to add social media links to your website and ask people to "like" your business page. Be sure to post new work at least once a week to keep people engaged. As of today, Facebook is THE most important online social media site.

Linked-In is a business social media site that should also be utilized in order to make connections—but you'll get business from this site as well. Be sure to connect with contacts at every type of business who may have events.

Twitter is used by almost everyone and is also a "must do." Twitter allows you to post short, up to 140 character statements which may include a link to your website. Every time you do something new, post a photo here.

Your Website:
A website is *the* most important and least expensive forms of advertising there is. And you can change it whenever you wish to keep up with new products and changes in your company. Now you don't need to know html in order to build a website—there are tools available that you can use and have a website published in one evening. www.godaddy.com us just one of the places you can go to use their online resources to build your

site with Web Builder, add photos and graphics, and publish your website by yourself. No expertise in html is needed, just a few hours of your time. If you prefer, turn the project over to a professional, but either way, do it now if you haven't already. So many people use the internet now that if you don't have a website it actually makes you look bad.

Be sure that your website has knockout pictures of your work (not anyone else's) and that it looks very professional. The more content the better. You may want to refer clients to your website to see samples of your work. Make sure your phone and email are on every page of your site so people can contact you easily.

Tips for good website design:

- Use modern, clean graphics

- Don't use music, or flashy or blinking graphics that are distracting

- Make sure your contact information is at the bottom of every page and on a contact page

- Place copyright information on the bottom of every page

- Be sure to use thumbnail photos on one page, then link them to larger photos

- Consider embedding photos with your company name so people will be less likely to use them on their own websites. This happens often in the balloon industry, so watch out for theft. Also never use anyone else's work on your website—only show your own. Some website hosts offer photo albums for you to use to store your photos and let customers browse through your designs.

- Use low resolution graphics for websites so the photos load faster. You can manipulate photos with a software program such as Adobe Photoshop Elements. Keep one copy of the low res photo for your website and one copy of a high res photo for printing in your computer files.

- Update your site at least once a month to keep it fresh.

- Consider adding a **Blog** to your website where you can showcase special projects, write articles, and customers can leave comments about your work.

- Backup your website to disk—you don't want to lose your hard work

- Use a submission service like ineedhits.com to submit your website to search engines on a monthly basis so people will be able to find you when they do searches. It is very important to have your site listed on Google, MSN, and Yuhoo which are the main internet search engines, but keeping up with it is very time consuming to do on your own.

How to Write a Press Release

Press Releases can be a useful tool to use to contact the media about an event that is newsworthy. Press releases can generate free publicity for your business or association. In order to create a release that will get the attention of the media, some guidelines must be kept in mind:

-The news must be "newsworthy." This means that you must have something new, different, unusual, or impressive. The newspapers, television stations, and radio stations get hundreds of press releases every day. Make your news stand out! Don't send a press release every month - only do a few per year
or the media will get tired of you and throw your messages out before reading them. Keep in mind that Non-Profit associations will get more consideration than individual companies, so if your balloon association is doing an event - be sure to send a press release to all of the local media. If

you want to advertise your business at the event, wear your company shirt with logo and park your van nearby.
-Try to develop a relationship with newspaper reporters. Your news is much more likely to get out if you have a personal relationship with reporters. You can meet reporters and editors at Chamber of Commerce meetings, political meetings, city council gatherings, etc. Take them to lunch and take the opportunity to let them know about your business.

-Keep the message short and to the point so it can be read quickly. News editors are very busy, and do not appreciate lengthy discussions. Be sure to include time, date, event, and location.

-Make sure to include all of your contact information so a reporter or editor can get in touch with you at any time. Include your cell-phone number and e-mail address. Reporters are often given assignments at the last minute and may need directions to your event or other information.

How to get the message out:

Research the internet under "state media" or "state newspapers," etc., and you will likely find a list of all of the media in your local area. At the very least, you will find a link to their websites. Write down their e-mail address, name, and company name and insert it into your e-mail address book. You can use this to mail to an address one time and place a statement at the bottom advising the recipient how to remove themselves from your mailing list. Be careful not to "spam" people with e-mail by sending out lots of ads.

Alternatively, take down the fax numbers and fax the press releases. Depending on what the event is, you may want to send one press release a few weeks ahead of time, and another a few days before the event. T.V. news is done on a last-minute basis, but they do appreciate a few days notice.

Also be sure to send a press release to your local newspapers, radio, and television stations at least a week in advance of the event. Do not send more than two press release to the same person about the same event!

Tip:

visit **www.prweb.com or** other press release sites, where you can write and send a press release out through the internet. PR Web also has press release guidelines to help you through the process.

Press Release Components

Title/Headline ➜ **Local Balloon Organization to do Balloon Release for Charity**

For Immediate Release ➜ For Immediate Release

Your city name and date ➜ (your city) (Date)

The first paragraph should include what you are doing, the date of the event, and who is involved ➜ A Nationwide Memorial Balloon Release will be held Friday, November 11, 2018 in remembrance of the Veterans who have served our country. Balloon organizations and others across the country will be participating.

The rest of the release should include details of the event, time, and location. ➜ The local Balloon Professionals Association will host a release using biodegradable balloons and no ribbons or plastic out of concern for the environment. The local event will be held at 11:00 a.m. at the Sharon Lane Nursing Center, (address). The chaplain from the center will perform a short ceremony before the release. The Hocker Grove Middle School, located directly across the street from the nursing center, will participate in the event, and their school band will play during the balloon release.

ACME Balloon Company of Salina, Kansas, is donating all of the red, white, and blue balloons, and Linweld,, Inc. of Independence, Missouri is donating the helium and tank delivery.
.
The Balloon Professionals Association is a non-profit educational group of local balloon decorators and entertainers. The association does at least one charitable event per year. Please contact *Name here*, president of the association at *phone here* or *e-mail address here* for questions.

Remember the five W's:

Who, What, Why, When, and Where

Be sure to include contact information so the media can contact you easily. ➜ Contact:
Mary Smith
Public Relations
BPA
phone
email

Logos, Trademarks, Copyrights and Patents

Logo and Trademarks

First, lets discuss your logo. A logo helps to "brand" your business and make you look more professional. It helps the consumer remember you, too. Every business should have a logo.

About logo infringement—don't copy someone else's logo and use it as your own. Think up something entirely different that says what you do in a picture or words. Software like "The Logo Creator," is available to make logos and help you come up with ideas, or hire a professional graphic artist to make one up for you. There are online services available at low cost.

If you have a trademark on your logo, this means that you are the only one who can use that logo in your state. Trademarks are applied for in EACH state, and you could get one in all 50 states in the U.S. if you wanted to, but some companies only have a trademarked logo in the states where the do business.

Just do an internet search for "Trademark" and your state name to find the website for application. This is usually found on the Secretary of State's website. The cost is usually low, it is approximately $50 for the application and $10 for annual renewal.

There is a Federal Trademark available, which covers all 50 states.

Copyright

Copyright protects a person from infringement on their ideas. If you put anything in print or in videos, including your website, it is a good idea to get a copyright from the U.S. Copyright office at **www.copyright.gov**. *Note: domain names cannot be copyrighted.* As of the printing of this book, the cost is $35.00 for written projects submitted online. However, you should also know that the minute you write something it is copyrighted, but proving that it was your idea first can be difficult. That is why anything important to you should be copyrighted officially. You can do it yourself easily.

Patents

If you design tools or equipment used in the balloon industry or other trades, you may want to consider getting a patent. If you want to sell the idea to a manufacturer, they won't even talk to you unless you already have a patent. And if they do, you run the risk of someone stealing the idea from you. If it is your first time to apply for a patent you may want some assistance with an attorney who is familiar with the process, or to save money do it yourself. This can be an expensive process and don't be surprised if it costs at least $5,000 to obtain a patent search and submit an application.

There are two types of patents you should know about: *Utility patents* may be granted to anyone who invents or discovers any new and useful process, machine, article of manufacture, or composition of matter, or any new and useful improvement. *Design patents* may be granted to anyone who invents a new, original, and ornamental design for an article of manufacture. Visit www.uspto.gov for more information on the patent process.

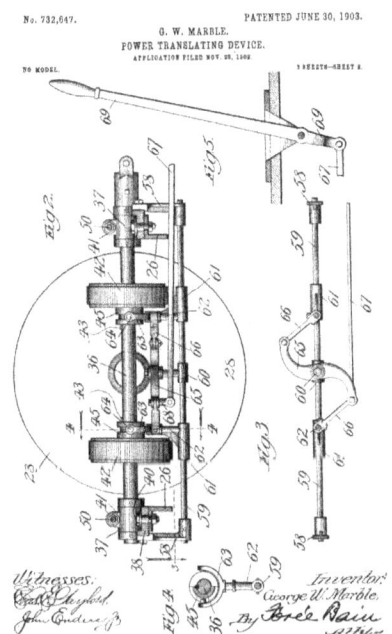

FIG. 936. A TYPICAL PATENT OFFICE DRAWING.

What You Need to Know About OSHA
United Stated Department of Labor Occupational Safety and Health Administration

OSHA has guidelines that must be followed for all workers and businesses. These are mandatory requirements. If your company is larger, you may have to keep safety logs and more.

- No children under age 16 are allowed on job sites, even in your vehicle, while you are working. Make arrangements for a babysitter if you have kids.
- No one outside the employ of the company or the owner of the site is allowed on a work site.
- No one under the age of 18 may use equipment, machinery, or climb ladders or scaffold, or install equipment. Basically, the only place a person under 18 can work in this industry is in the office.
- Be sure to follow all OSHA recommendations for ladder safety, climbing, working on roofs, fall protection, lifting, etc. You can get these from your worker's comp carrier, from a safety company, or at regional and national conventions and classes.
- You must have a safety manual and Material Safety Data Sheets in all vehicles at all times.
- Your employee manual must have a statement requiring adherence to all safety rules (eye protection, ear protection, fall protection, head protection, etc.) WITH consequences for failure to comply. If the person does not comply he/she should be subject to suspension or termination.
- All accidental deaths or severe injuries must be reported to OSHA immediately.
- Recordkeeping must be completed by companies with more than 10 employees. Keep a record of all injuries in a log book.
- A Safety Coordinator must be assigned.
- Regular safety meetings must be held for employees. I suggest one per week. You can obtain safety meeting ideas from safety companies online. Have everyone sign a log after each meeting.
- All new hires need to have safety training.
- A clearly marked area for safety gear and first aid kit must be on all trucks.

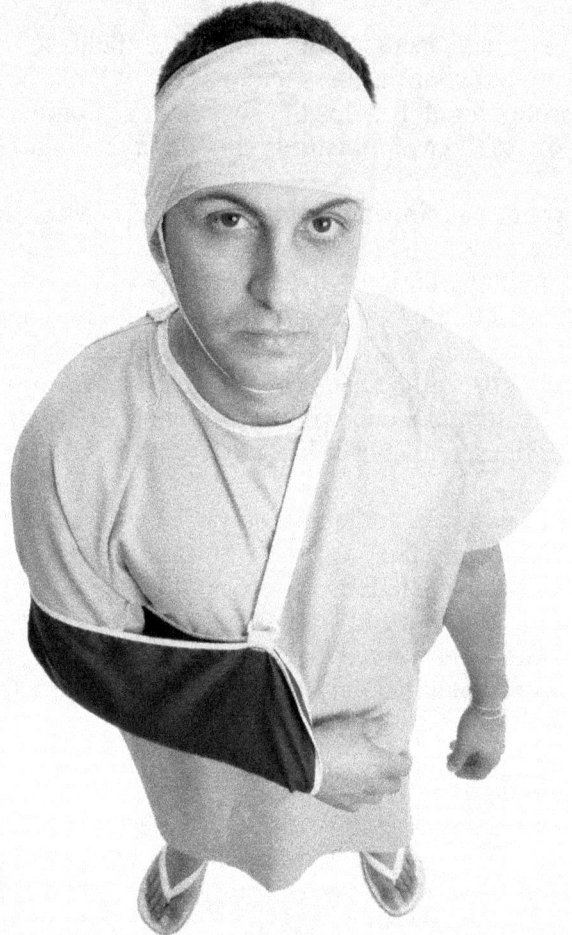

Fall Protection

Falls are the leading cause of death among construction accidents with approximately 362 deaths per year. Don't let you or your employees take unnecessary risks.

- When above six feet in height fall protection is necessary.
- If you step off of a ladder to perform a task, fall protection is necessary in the form of a harness or scaffold with safety railings.
- Do not attempt to install flue liners, clay pots, or do masonry restoration without scaffolding and safety rails as required by OSHA. Charge your client accordingly.

Personal Protective Equipment

Your field employees will need the following on hand, and use them when needed:

- **Ear protection** (ear plugs or over the ear protectors). If you want to keep your hearing, use them!
- **Eye protection** (approved safety glasses) I suggest the type that cover your eyes completely on all sides. Small shards of metal or wood can fly in and cause serious damage. An ulcerated eye is painful and can cause blindness.
- **Lung protection** Dust mask, full face mask. Use anytime dust is created or organic vapors are present, when using a saw, sweeping a chimney, etc.
- **Fall protection:** Personal harness system (if applicable).

Keep personal protective gear in a safe place such as a box that will keep them undamaged and without scratches. Clearly mark the box with the employee's name on it. The employer is required to provide all protective gear for each employee—no sharing allowed.

Be ready for a random site inspection anytime because OSHA inspectors do drive around towns and cities looking for job sites. This happened to several contractors I know personally and they ALL had violations and heavy fines. While it may be impossible to avoid violations, if you make a conscious effort to follow the laws and regulations they inspector will see that and may go easier on you.

Take an OSHA approved training course, and take all of your employees with you. At the end of this course you will know what you need to do to be OSHA Compliant and set up a safety coordinator, manual (see the safety manual in this book for more ideas), personal protective equipment, fall protection, how to erect scaffold, and much more. Certified training companies offer this course, OSHA does not. An internet search under "OSHA Certified Trainer" will give you a list of sources.

For more information:

Occupational Safety & Health Administration
U.S. Department of Labor
200 Constitution Avenue
Washington, D.C. 20210
800-321-OSHA (6742)... TTY 1-877-889-5627
Visit **www.osha.gov** for more information

If you have an **EMERGENCY**
(EX: to report a fatality or imminent life threatening situation)
Call this toll free number immediately:
1-800-321-OSHA (6742)
TTY 1-877-889-5627

Tip:

If you keep a safety manual, have regular safety training, and report accidents in a timely manner, you are much less likely to be hit with a large fine if something happens.

For questions concerning the child labor laws, contact the Employment Standards Administration's Wage and Hour Division (WHD). www.youthrules.dol.gov/jobs.htm

The Fair Labor Standards Act (Fair Labor Standards Act (FLSA)) sets wage, hours worked, and safety requirements for minors (individuals under age 18) working in jobs covered by the statute. All states have child labor standards.

Making a Profit in the Balloon Industry

Why do people get into this business? There are usually three reasons: 1. They grew up in it with their parents and want to continue the business.. 2. They really love doing this kind of work. 3. They want to make a living (i.e. profit) doing this kind of work because they love it.

Whatever your reason is for starting your own business, an often overlooked factor is actually making a profit doing what you love. And its not easy, not for a balloon business or for any other type of business. The time frame to make a profit in most businesses is five years. After that, the company should be well established, have returning customers, and be well known in their market.

However, if you have previous business experience and know the ropes, the time frame for making a profit with your new business could be shortened to two or three years.

I've owned a number of businesses over the years including a chimney and fireplace contracting company for over 35 years, a forensic investigation company for 19 years, a balloon décor company for 10 years, a publishing company (and writing books) for 20 years, and now a new real estate investment company which is going gangbusters. But it wasn't always that way. I made bad decisions, have opened and closed three retail stores because I found out that I simply did not like retail, and they were in the wrong location. Essentially, I know how to make a profit, and how to not make a profit. So I hope you'll pay attention to this chapter so you will avoid the same mistakes I did, and hopefully, gain insight from my successes.

The biggest problem by far in the balloon entertainment or décor industry is that some people consider this a hobby, rather than a business. As a hobbyist, the person is not interested in making money at all—they simply have so much fun making other people happy that they'll do it, even for free. And that is fine when you are doing work for your family and friends, or even your club or church.

But when the hobbyist decides to make the transition to balloon business owner, this is where it gets tricky. Your friends and family no longer want to pay for your services. And the hobbyist transitioning to business owner usually (not always) does not have a clue as to how to charge for their services.

All business owners need to do two things to be successful: Know your business and know how to run a business.

Know your Business
Before doing any work that you get paid for, attend workshops, conventions, and meetings, and get as much training in the technical part as possible, until you feel comfortable that you are a real professional and can train others to do what you have learned.

Check the internet for local clubs, and regional and national conferences. At the big conferences you can learn a lot in just a few days from many experts in the industry. Be sure to take notes and lots of photos.

Practice doing what you have learned at home or for friends and family and take lots of pictures. Critique yourself to be sure that the design work looks professional. If it does, keep the photos to

Showcase later on your website and in your portfolio that you will be showing potential clients.

Check the list of resources in the back of this book for more information.

Know How to Run a Business

This is the part that most balloon artists and entertainers find difficult. Most people are either right brained (creative) or left-brained (analytical), and therefore are not so well suited to handling the finances, marketing, web design, and day to day operations if they are right-brained. I assume that the reader is right-brained or you wouldn't be in the business of balloons.

So what to do? Either get a partner, or hire someone to do this type of work. It usually does take two people to manage any type of service business, one in the office, the other in the field. And believe me, the balloon business is a service business. You are serving clients, doing a professional job, and getting paid to do it. Your clients view your service as any number of other types of companies they hire for events such as florists, caterers, and D.J's. They want all of it to be perfect, completed on time, and they want to deal with a pro every time.

Whoever the left brainer is, make sure they either have had a lot of experience running a business or get them the training they need. Taking business courses at a local college or private trainer may be necessary. This person needs to know accounting, how to run a program such as Quick Books Pro (the one I use), do payroll, taxes, invoicing, manage insurance policies, take employment applications, and manage a bank account. You may also assign this person the job of ordering supplies that will be needed for jobs. This is usually a full-time job, so don't plan on being both the field person and the office manager.

FREE business advise is available for any small business from SCORE at www.score.org Score has information about business plans, workshops, marketing, finances, and technology and is a great resource.

Pricing: The number one thing that puts most companies in this industry out of business is not knowing how to price their jobs properly. If you don't price correctly, you will not be in business a year from now, guaranteed. There are several standard rules for pricing that apply to any type of service business.

How to Price Your Services

Take these things into consideration:

1. Figure the cost of supplies and materials for a job, allowing 10% overage for loss or breakage.

2. Figure the cost of gas (helium or nitrogen)

3. Figure the cost of all of your equipment purchased and divide it by 250. (allotting two weeks off for vacation time) If you ever have repairs or replacement parts, add that cost in to the total equipment cost for the year. Now you have the cost per day for your equipment.

4. Figure the average cost for your vehicles used in the business, plus repairs and maintenance, for the year and divide by 250.

5. Labor costs: Take your total payroll cost for the year, including taxes paid by the company and health insurance or other benefits. Include your own salary (and you'd better be paying yourself a salary!) and once again divide by 250 to see the weekly price.

6. Fixed expenses: Insurance costs for workers comp and liability, rent, utilities, dues and subscriptions, education, travel, etc.

7. Advertising: including networking luncheons or dinners, website hosting and design, print ads, radio ads, signage or wraps for vehicles, business cards, printed uniforms, photos, portfolio, etc. Note: Advertising should cost no more than 10% of your total gross income.

See the next page for a sample job cost form

Sample Job Cost Form for a Balloon Décor Job

This is just a sample—you will need to input your own prices. I suggest using a program such as Excel.

Materials/Supplies	Price	Quantity	Total
11" pearl white balloons	14.65 for 100	3	43.95
11" pearl black balloons	14.65 for 100	3	43.95
5" pearl white balloons	6.40 for 100	3	19.20
5" pearl black balloons	6.40 for 100	3	19.20
11" Damask pearl wht/ black ink	12.80 for 50/bag	2	25.60
Zebra ribbon 1/4" 200 yds	4.50 for 200 yds	2	9.00
Black ribbon 3/8"	2.35 for 250 yd	2	4.70
Hi-float pump kit	12.95	1	12.95
Premade weights	5.95	30	178.50
Helium	45.00	1	45.00
		Total material costs:	$402.05
	Retail markup	x 1.66 =	$667.32
OVERHEAD COSTS		Shipping	24.00
*Equipment costs	Per day average	35	35.00
**Fixed Overhead	Per day average	135.00	135.00
Labor $15 hr	120 ea per 8 hr day	4 people	480.00
Owner Salary	193.00 per day	193	193.00
**Vehicle expense	.58 per mile per vehicle	16 miles	9.28
		Total overhead costs:	$841.28
		Markup 30% =	$252.38
		Materials =	$667.32
		Tax on materials =	$48.38
		Total job price =	$1,809.36

Sample Job Cost Form for a Balloon Entertainer Job

This is just a sample—you will need to input your own prices. I suggest using a program such as Excel.

Materials/Supplies	Price	Quantity	Total
260Q balloons Red	6.60 for 100	1/2 bag	3.30
260Q balloons Blue	6.60 for 100	1/2 bag	3.30
260Q balloons White	6.60 for 100	1	6.60
160Q balloons Asst	5.90	1	5.90
		Total material costs:	$19.10
	Retail markup	x 1.66 =	$31.70
OVERHEAD COSTS		Shipping	15.00
*Equipment costs	Per day average		2.60
**Fixed Overhead	Per day average	135.00	135.00
Labor $15 hr	120 ea per 8 hr day	2 people	240.00
Owner Salary	193.00 per day	193	193.00
**Vehicle expense	.58 per mile per vehicle	16 miles	9.28
		Total overhead costs:	$626.59
		Markup 30% =	$189.97
		Total job price =	$816.56

Charge more if you wish to make a bigger profit

Tip: Figure your total price based on an 8–hour day even if the job is only for a half day. You must have a minimum per day to operate. Otherwise, schedule two jobs a day to fill the day.

*Equipment costs	Per day average	1	35.00
**Fixed Overhead	Per day average	135.00	135.00
Labor $15 hr	120 ea per 8 hr day	4 people	480.00
Owner Salary	193.00 per day	1	193.00
***Vehicle expense	.58 per mile per vehicle	16 miles	9.28

* Equipment costs. In the above example balloon décor job the equipment costs includes the cost of all of your equipment, maintenance, and replacement for one year, divide by 50 to get your weekly cost. Be sure to include the full weekly cost in the estimate if you only do one job a week.

** Fixed Overhead. This includes the following:
- Rent
- Utilities
- Liability insurance
- Workers Comp insurance
- Taxes
- Office staff
- Legal and professional fees
- Cost of vehicles used for business only
- Other fixed expenses

*** Vehicle expense. Vehicle expense covers maintenance on the vehicle such as repairs and oil changes, and gas. .58 per mile is the amount allowed by the IRS.

The owner salary in this case is $50,000 per year, so change this as needed. If you have a partner, figure the cost of both salaries in the equation. The cost per day is based on a 5-day week for 50 weeks, allotting for vacation time. If you are not paying yourself a salary yet, plan to do so because you need to make money, too!

The profit margin was figures at 30%, but many companies figure this at 50% to allow for extra unforeseen costs, and to improve their bottom line.

You may want to establish a job minimum—meaning the smallest amount you will accept to do a job. The smaller jobs just don't make much

Tip:

If you would prefer to use your own personal vehicle for business use, you may pay yourself .58 per mile. Keep good records of your personal and business use of the vehicle and give this information to your accountant.

You may also deduct the portion of your home used for business only -such as an office or storage area.

sense for balloon decorators because once you factor in the time and effort needed to plan, order materials, load up tanks and equipment drive to the site, and do the work, you may actually loose money.

For balloon entertainers who do not have large overhead expenses and equipment, and are often one-or two man operations, a lower job minimum can work.

The Professional Proposal

I started writing contracts and proposals in 1982 when my husband began a chimney sweep business. I soon learned that I didn't know much about contracts, so had to seek out books and seminars on the subject. Later, when working on my own balloon business I found that there were even more things I needed to include in order to protect myself and the client. So I've compiled the most important items for the balloon decorator or entertainer here.

The following are suggestions for items to include in your proposal:

1.) A Cover Letter thanking the client for the opportunity to work with them on their project.

2.) The Proposal/ Contract
    a. Provide a very detailed description (typed only so you know it can be read by the client) of the work you are proposing. Remember that the client cannot visualize as you can and needs as much help as possible. Detail will also prevent any misunderstandings about what you will provide.

    b. Add drawings or photos to help the client visualize better.

    c. Use only 12 or 14 point type so your proposal is is easy to read. Use a legal size 8 1/2" x 14" paper if necessary, or additional pages.

3.) Provide **references** and information about your company up front, or mention in your letter that references are available.

4.) Offer to provide a **certificate of insurance** for your liability (minimum 1 million coverage) and workers comp. Some companies will also require proof of auto insurance if you work on their property.

5.) Provide at least one **photo** of your past work related to their job even if the person you met with has already seen it. In the case of a corpo-
rate job, another group of people will see your proposal and likely have not seen photos of your work. If you are just getting started and don't have many photos—do a party for yourself or a friend and get some good photos of your work. *Hint: Don't tackle corporate jobs until you have some experience in the business.*

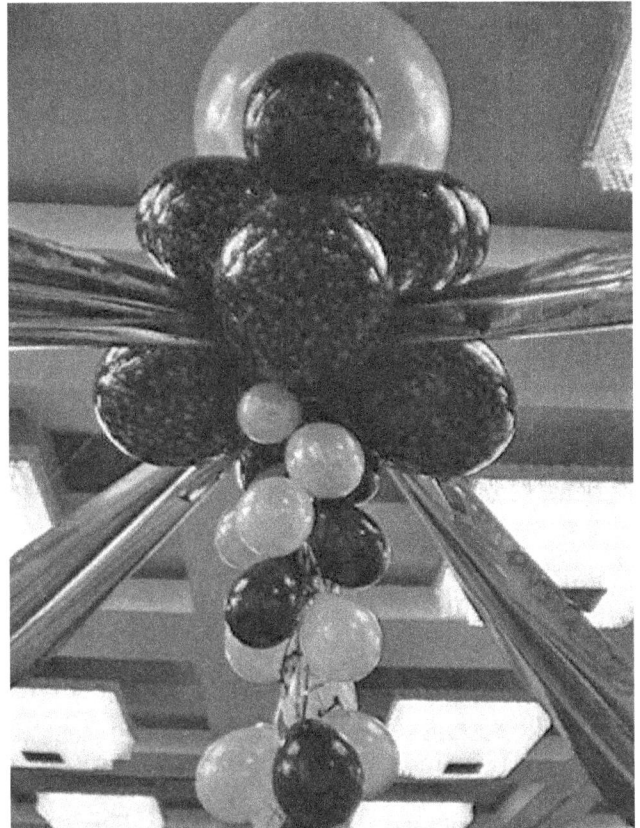

6.) Include your **business card** in the proposal. Make sure to put your e-mail and web address on business cards, letterheads, and proposals.

7.) Add a **color brochure** to give your client ideas for the future. The client will likely keep this on hand and call you back next time! It will also give them ideas for other events.

8.) Be sure to follow up every job with a "**thank you**" postcard, letter, or phone call. For larger jobs a gift or flowers may be in order. This extra touch shows your professionalism. You might want to send corporate clients another business card or rolodex card to keep on hand for easy reference.

The Contract

The following contracts are samples that you may want to use in your business. Although they have been checked by an attorney, you may want to have your own attorney look them over to see if anything different applies in your state. Please read the contracts thoroughly to see if everything applies to you, and if not, change them accordingly.

Some of the clauses may be left out of contracts— such as the weather clause to be used for outdoor work only. I would suggest that certain things be included in any contract:

- A contingency clause for "Plan B" in case the venue needs to be changed

- For outdoor events, a "Plan B" indoor site option in case of inclement weather with notice required 24 hours in advance of the event.

- Make certain the exact time and date of the event is included in the contract

- Be sure to include the time you and your crew will arrive to begin work

- Be sure to tell the client that they are responsible for your gaining access to the venue at the agreed time and for providing electricity

- Get contact information for the site manager, who may not be the client, who is your "go to" person during your set up time.

- Mention that the venue must have air conditioning or heat set to a comfortable level at the time you arrive with your crew

- Carefully describe the décor you are planning to use, with exact colors and types of balloons or other items, and include the number of each that will be included.

- Mention that if access to the venue is not available upon arrival, that the client is still responsible for payment in full even if it is not completed at the stated time.

- Include sample photos or drawings so the client can visualize the end result.

Use these ideas at your own discretion. I made the following contracts, using Microsoft Publisher, but you can use any word processor to make the same type of design. Be sure to include a signature line at the bottom of EACH page for your customer to sign, so you have proof that they read the entire contract. Keep the original copy for yourself and provide a copy for your client. You may want to use Docusign at docusign.com, which is easier for the client, and is considered to be a legal document.

☞ *Tip:*

Make up as many décor items as possible the day before the event, and place in plastic bags to keep the balloons looking fresh. Include weights, centerpieces, and all air or nitrogen filled balloons. This goes for balloon entertainers as well, who may want to have several creations made up ahead of time for larger events.

The Best Balloon Company

Decorators Sample

77 Lucky Drive, Balloonville, USA 90210
800-555-1212
FAX 811-555-1313
e-mail: Thebest@gmail.com
Website: Thebestballoons.com

Customer Name:	
Address:	
Phone:	
Fax:	

PROPOSAL/CONTRACT

Date: _____
Event date and time: _____

WE HEREBY PROPOSE TO PROVIDE THE FOLLOWING: *(Note: This proposal is confidential. Our design ideas are copyrighted and may not be shared with other decorators.)*

[] **1.) Room Decor-** Nine 50 foot wide x 20 foot tall pearl arches using 16" silver and sapphire blue latex balloons, with one 3' silver foil star balloon in the center, with shiny mylar ribbons and balloon squiggles attached to each balloon. These will be attached to the side wires in the hall and across the entire center of the area between hanging lights. The arches will be evenly spaced.

[] **2.) Stage -** four clusters (one placed on each corner of the stage) with one 3' silver or blue foil star and nine 16" helium latex dark blue balloons underneath them attached to a mylar weight. These will be raised up high so guests can see the stage.

[] **3.) Entrance arch** over the doorway - a pearl arch made with 16" silver and dark blue latex balloons and shiny ribbons.

[] **4.) Registration:** We will place two bouquets with nine 11" latex balloons and one 18" foil star balloon arranged in a stacked pattern on top placed on the floor on either side of the registration table.

[] **5.) Guest Tables:** A balloon-covered round board with small 3" silver and blue latex balloons, 4" foil stars balloons, mylar tufts, and ting-ting (see photo). Total height- 30". Total centerpieces = 50

Arrival: We will arrive at the event site at 8:00 A.M. on _____ and will complete the job by 5:30 P.M.

Utilities: We must have access to electricity and lighting in order to work. The temperature in the hall must be between 68 and 75 degrees so the décor work will look it's best. Temperatures that are too different than those during the event may cause balloons to shrink or expand and the décor will not look as nice as possible.

Continued on next page...

Acceptance of Proposal: (Please sign at the bottom of each page, return one copy of this proposal, and keep one copy for your records) The above prices, specifications and conditions are satisfactory and are hereby accepted. You are authorized to do the work as specified. Payment will be made as outlined above.

Accepted by: Signature_____ Date _____

Title _____ Printed name _____

(Page 2 of 2)
Proposal to _____ Continued.

The Best Balloon Company

Terms: 30% non-refundable retainer is required to hold the date with balance due two weeks before the event. $1,500.00 decor minimum order for events in our service area, $3,000.00 minimum for out-of-town events. *Framework and rental items must be returned to our office within three days of the event.* We do not tear down unless so stated in the proposal. We will provide boxes to put these items in, and a list of items to return. *The Best Balloon Company* will not install any balloon decor if other balloons are present which are not installed or supervised by *The Best Balloon Company.*

Guarantee: If decor is not completed on time, and it is due to our negligence, you will be refunded for the portion not completed. However, we are not responsible for uncompleted decor if we are not allowed into a facility or met by the assigned person at the time arranged and it delays our work. We will do the work agreed upon in this proposal. Last minute changes are at our discretion based on availability of materials and time. No refunds for any part of the contract that the client wishes not to use the day of the event.

Person responsible for allowing us entrance to the facility: _____

Phone number and cell phone: _____

A separate refundable deposit of $500 is required for rental items: electrical extension cords, lighting, and framework. This will be refunded upon the safe return of these items.

We Hereby Propose to furnish labor and materials complete in accordance with the above specifications for the amount of **$X,XXX.XX, with payment to be made as follows: 30% retainer ($XXXX.XX) due at time of order, with balance due two weeks before the event.** If the balance is not received by the due date, the contract is subject to cancellation. All material is guaranteed to be as specified unless a supplier makes it unavailable. In that case, we reserve the right to substitute an item of like kind and quality. The earlier the order is placed, the better chance we have of getting your choice of materials. Do not let small children put latex balloons in their mouths. We are not responsible for accidents or injuries related to our decor that is mishandled by the client or site staff. Completion of the job contingent upon access to the event site at the time arranged.

Inclement Weather: No refunds for outdoor work due to inclement weather, or damage to décor once it is completed. We *strongly* suggest an alternate site arrangement for outdoor work, but we must be notified of the location of the alternate site one weeks ahead of the event date, and we must be notified of the final decision for the location at least four hours prior to our arrival time. Note: temperatures over 85° will cause helium to escape balloons quickly. All balloons oxidize (get a velvety coating) outside, but that does not change the color of the balloons. Hot weather may cause foil balloon to pop. Wind can loosen designs. Cold weather may cause balloons to shrink.

Subcontractors/Rentals: If we hire subcontractors or rent equipment, the customer is responsible for additional charges for labor due to delays or time changes beyond our control. Additionally, if we are not allowed access to the site for any reason, the customer will be responsible for extra charges incurred for labor.

Removal of Decor: We do not remove decorations from the site unless so stated in the proposal. We will leave instructions for tear down with the responsible party, and will include instructions with this contract.

Payment: Price good for 60 days. Payment may be made with MasterCard, Visa, Discover, cash, check, or money order. Final payment must be received at the time indicated above, or your reservation may be revoked.

Authorized by: _____ (your name) Date _____

Acceptance of Proposal: (Please sign and return one copy of this proposal, and keep one copy for your records) The above prices, specifications and conditions are satisfactory and are hereby accepted. You are authorized to do the work as specified. Payment will be made as outlined above.

Accepted by: Signature_____ Date _____

Title _____ Printed name _____

B-B's Balloons

Entertainer's Sample

Customer Name:	
Address:	
Phone:	
Fax:	

PROPOSAL/CONTRACT

777 Lucky Drive, Balloonville, USA 90210
800-555-1212
FAX 811-555-1313
e-mail: Thebest@earthlink.net
Website: Thebestballoons.com

Date: _____
Event date and time: _____

WE HEREBY PROPOSE TO PROVIDE THE FOLLOWING:
(Note: This proposal is confidential.)

1.) We shall provide one entertainer near the registration desk and one entertainer at the center of the main hall. Each person will wear a costume and will make balloon animals, flowers, and toys while entertaining the crowd. tems will be given to persons attending the function.

2.) Work time period: I (we) shall work at the designated area for the period from 3:00 P.M. to 7:00 P.M. with a 10-minute break each hour.

Payment: The client shall pay $XXX for each entertainer ($XXX total), and entertainers keep all tips.

Terms: 30% non-refundable retainer is required to hold the date with balance due two weeks before the event. $800.00 minimum order for events in _____, $1,500.00 minimum order for out-of-town events.

Guarantee: If we do not arrive at the scheduled time due to our negligence, you will receive a refund for the time period we did not work. However, we are not responsible if we are not allowed into a facility or met by the assigned person at the time arranged and it delays our work, or for cancellations due to weather or other reasons. We will do the work agreed upon in this proposal. Last minute additional time changes are at our discretion based on availability of materials and time.

Person responsible for allowing us entrance to the facility: _____
Phone and cell numbers: _____

We Hereby Propose to furnish labor and materials complete in accordance with the above specifications for the amount of **$X,XXX.XX, with payment to be made as follows: 30% retainer ($XXXX.XX) due at time of order, with balance due two weeks before the event.** If the balance is not received by the due date, the contract is subject to cancellation. We are not responsible for accidents or injuries related to balloons that is mishandled by the client or site staff. Small children should be supervised with balloons and should keep balloons out of their mouths. Completion of the job contingent upon access to the event site at the time arranged.

Acceptance of Proposal: (Please sign and return one copy of this proposal, and keep one copy for your records) The above prices, specifications and conditions are satisfactory and are hereby accepted. You are authorized to do the work as specified. Payment will be made as outlined above.

Accepted by: Signature_____ Date _____
Title _____ Printed name _____

(page 1 of 2) Proposal continued...

B-B's Balloons

1234 Main St.,
Los Angeles, CA, USA 90210
800-555-1212 FAX 811-555-1313
e-mail: Thebest@earthlink.net
Website: Thebestballoons.com

Customer Name:	
Address:	
Phone:	
Fax:	

PROPOSAL/CONTRACT

Date: _____
Event date and time: _____

Inclement Weather: No refunds for outdoor work due to inclement weather. We *strongly* suggest an alternate site arrangement for outdoor work, but we must be notified of the location of the alternate site one week ahead of the event date. We must be notified of the final decision at least four hours prior to our arrival time.

Customer is responsible for the behavior of attendees, and if any attendee becomes abusive to our entertainers, the customer agrees to ask them to leave the area.

Authorized by: _____ (your name) Date _____

Acceptance of Proposal: (Please sign and return one copy of this proposal, and keep one copy for your records) The above prices, specifications and conditions are satisfactory and are hereby accepted. You are authorized to do the work as specified. Payment will be made as outlined above.

Accepted by: Signature_____ Date _____

Title _____ Printed name _____

Tips To Keep Out of Trouble

• Be On Time

Make sure that you leave for every job early. Provide alarm clocks or wake-up calls for employees if necessary. Always be early—never late! And have enough help to finish your jobs ahead of the scheduled time to finish. Estimate 1 hour later than you really plan to be done so the client is not breathing down your back to finish up.

• Get a Signed Contract

Be sure to get a signed contract and payment in full BEFORE starting a job— you'll be glad you did. Never do a job without a contract—you could be setting yourself up for trouble if you don't have a contract. People have been sued for not doing what they said they would do verbally, so don't let that happen to you! Additionally, your state may require you to have a written contract by law for any work done for a customer.

• Be Firm

If something goes wrong that is not your fault—such as a lift not being provided by the client when it was stated so in the contract, be firm about your contract and do not give a refund. You paid for supplies and labor for the day, and could have booked another job in place of the one that had a problem, so you would lose income.

• Who is In Charge?

Have the person in charge make sure to introduce themselves to the coordinator of the event immediately upon arrival so they know who to talk to about the arrangements.

• Dress Professionally

Employees should all wear the same color pants and a company shirt– except for the owner or person in charge of the event, who should also wear a vest or jacket to identify them as the person of authority. Make sure that everyone has a name tag that identifies them by name and position, including yourself. Plastic printed tags that pin on shirts are available at office supply stores and printers online.

• Order Supplies Early

As soon as you have a contract and the down-payment, make a list of supplies and order them. Place supplies in a box or boxes with the job name and date on it– and when everything is collected, put a sign on the box that says "ready." Always check helium and nitrogen tanks when they arrive—sometimes they arrive empty!

• Make a Weekly/Monthly Schedule

Be sure to keep all jobs on scheduling software or written by hand in a schedule book so you never miss an important job.

Celebrations Balloon Company, Inc.

1234 S Main St, New York, New York 50049

May 20, 2020

(2 –3spaces after date)
Ms. Jackie Franklin
Event Coordinator
Trump Industries, Inc.
350 E 10th Street
New York, NY 50046
(2-3 spaces after address)

<table>
<tr><td>***Sample Letter***
in standard business format

Note that all of your contact information and logo should be on your letterhead for a professional look and to make it easy for your client to contact you.</td></tr>
</table>

Dear Ms. Franklin: *(use a colon)*
(2 spaces after salutation)

It was nice meeting you on Tuesday. Thank you for the opportunity to provide décor ideas and a quotation for décor for your banquet on November 20th at the Ritz Carlton.

Enclosed are some sketches of ideas we have for the table centerpieces, buffet arrangements, stage décor, and room entrance décor as we discussed, along with a proposal and pricing. The cost is under your budget of $10,000. I am confident that you will find our staff professional and courteous, and that you will be very happy with the results. We want your event to be fun and exciting just as much as you do, and we know that the décor is a very important part of the experience your guests will have.

If you would like to schedule the work, please sign the contract and send it in with a check for the retainer. Please contact me if you have any questions about this proposal.

(Three spaces)
Sincerely,

(Four spaces)

Mary Wilson, CBA

SAMPLE LETTER TO CLIENT

Your Employee Manual

All businesses need an employee manual so that everyone in the company knows the rules and procedures of your business. This not only helps the employee understand your policies, but it is important for the employer to have this as a reference guide as well. Making your own employee manual will require you to think about what you expect of your employees and what benefits you should (or can) offer.

Revise your manual once per year to make any changes that may happen regarding health insurance or policies.

The following employee manual is an example of what I have used in our business which may be helpful to you in creating your own manual. I update our manual annually, or whenever we add or subtract something, such as a new benefit, or loss of a benefit, and give a new copy to all employees. We also have an annual meeting to discuss changes to the manual so that everyone knows what to expect and is reminded about our company rules. The manual is also one of the discussion points with all new hires, and they must sign a form saying that they have read and agree to the terms in the manual..

You may want to have a copy of the employee manual out on top of a desk in your office so employees can refer to it as needed.

Go through the following manual, and add or remove items as you desire.

Sample Employee Manual

A. Benefits

1. **Paid Holidays:** All **full-time** hourly employees who have been employed with the company for at least three months receive four paid holidays per year: Independence Day, Thanksgiving day, Christmas day, and New Year's Day. f a paid holiday falls on a weekend, we take the next Monday off. In addition, we have two unpaid holidays: Memorial Day, and Labor Day. We work all other holidays unless they fall on the weekend.

2. **Vacation:** A one-week paid vacation is available to all full and part-time hourly employees who have been with the company for at least one year, and is based on the average weekly pay for the previous 12 months. After employees have been employed continuously with the company for a period of five years, a two-week paid vacation will be provided. All vacations must be taken between December 26 and July 31. No vacations are allowed between August 1 and December 24.

4. **Sick Days: Full-time** Employees may take up to three personal or sick days per year after six months of service. If ill for more than one day at a time, a doctor's excuse must be provided. Days off for other reasons must be submitted at least two weeks in advance and approved by an officer. Sick days are unpaid.

3. **Pension plan.** All employees are eligible to participate in the company pension plan, if offered, after one month of employment. The company will match up to 3% of the employee's salary for any amount that the employee also contributes (1%, 2% or 3%). The employee may choose to contribute more on his/her own if desired.

4. **Accident policy through Colonial or Aflac:** his is paid on your own and you pay for it with pre-tax dollars, which lowers the cost for you. If you have an accidental injury on or off of work, you will receive benefits. This is OPTIONAL. Ask the office manager about the program.

5. **Life insurance:** All full-time employees receive a $50,000 life insurance policy from the company through our health insurance plan after three months of employment. This is subject to change if we change health providers.

6. **Employee Discount:** Employees may purchase small items for their own use (i.e. their child's birthday party) at our wholesale price plus shipping on all retail items and accessories such as latex or foil balloons.

7. **Workmen's Compensation Insurance:** All employees are covered under our Workmen's Compensation Insurance Plan for injuries sustained on the job. Injuries must be reported to a supervisor or to the office IMMEDIATELYAFTER THE ACCIDENT OR IT WILL NOT BE COVERED BY THE PLAN. **Safety:** All employees must adhere to safety guidelines when using equipment. Follow proper procedure for use of all equipment as instructed during training. Improper use of equipment may *disqualify* you for receiving benefits from insurance. Employees should war masks provide d when dust is created, and must wear a respirator during chimney cleaning or repair when dust or soot is created, and wear a safety harness where required. Also see the attached safety policy.

8. **Pre-Tax plan:** Any benefits that the employee pays for are pre-tax under our section 125 Cafeteria plan. This means that you will take home more pay than if this was not in effect.

Employee Benefits, Continued

10. Health Insurance— Full-Time employees:
The company currently pays for 50% of the employee's major medical health insurance plan, which includes a vision policy, doctor's visits, and prescription drugs. There are copays—which change annually. Employees are eligible for insurance after three months of full-time employment (30 hours or more per week). This is optional. If you already have a health plan through your spouse's employer, or other source, you do not need to enroll. Employees may add family members at their own expense if desired. The current plan is with United Health Care. These terms are subject to change based on availability and price of plans.

11. Pay dates: All payroll checks are distributed at 5:00 p.m. on Friday, for the previous week ending on Saturday. Sunday is considered the start day of the new week.

B. Company Rules

Absolutely No Smoking
1.) In our vehicles
2.) On the job site while working
3.) In the office

Eye Protection
Employees **must** wear eye protection when blowing up 3' or larger latex balloons, working with glitter, or any product that could harm the eyes.

Ear Protection
Employees **must** wear ear protection (provided by the company) when using or when near noisy equipment such as electric inflators. Ear protection should be worn if you cannot hear someone talking to you at arm's length. Permanent hearing loss may occur if ear protection is not worn.

Clothing:
OSHA requires that long pants, shirts tucked in, and no jewelry be worn on the job. Long hair must be pulled back and secured. There can be nothing on your person that could cause you to become entangled in equipment and cause injury. The company will provide uniforms. You are required to wear only our uniform on the job and to keep uniforms clean. Wash them in cold water for longer-lasting wear.

The company will provide head, eye and ear protection. Keep these items in their boxes to keep them clean and safe from scratches (required by OSHA).

Safety Manual
Each vehicle has a safety manual, MSDS sheets, and instructions in case of an accident. Read the manual and use it when needed. Employees must read our safety manual, attend safety meetings, and follow instructions by the supervisor regarding our procedures and safety methods.

Under the Influence:
Any employee found to be under the influence of drugs or alcohol while on the job will be immediately terminated. This is for your safety and the safety of others. Periodic drug testing may be implemented at any time and is required just after any type of accident, including vehicular accidents.

C. Company Policy Rules

Sexual Harassment:
Pursuant to current laws, the company must include this policy. No sexual harassment of fellow employees, male or female, in any manner whatsoever will be tolerated, and may result in a warning, suspension, or termination depending on the severity of the offense.

First Aid/CPR training:
All employees who work in the field must be First Aid/CPR Certified by the Red Cross and carry your card with you at all times. The company will provide the training every three years.

Probationary Period:
All new hires are under a four-week probationary period. After that time, we will evaluate the work performance and determine if the employee is to be offered a permanent position.

Absences/Tardiness
All employees are important to the operation of the company. When someone is late or absent, it puts all of our work behind schedule and creates scheduling problems, delays in payment for contracts, etc. You are expected to show up on time every day and work a full day without interruptions except for scheduled breaks and lunch. If late or absent three times within one year, you will receive a warning. If you are going to be absent due to illness or emergency, call the office first thing in the morning to let us know. If you do not call in you will receive a warning. If absent due to illness, we need a doctor's excuse when you return. Excessive tardiness or absences will result in termination.

Phones
Our phones are for company use only, and are to be available at all times. The supervisor or crew leader should have the company cell phone on his person at all times so we can contact him/her. No personal phone calls are allowed during working hours unless for an emergency, and this includes use of your own cell phone. You may make personal phone calls during break times. Do not talk on the phone or text while driving.

Uniforms
Employees will be furnished with hats and shirts. Please wash the shirts daily and come to work clean. Wear your own black work pants or jeans during cold months and tan or light colored pants during warm months. No shorts are allowed—if you are injured because you wear shorts we are not responsible for your injury. All employees MUST wear our company uniforms—no other attire is acceptable and you will be sent home if you are not in uniform.

Transportation
All employees must have reliable transportation to and from work every day. You will be docked in pay if you are late, or make anyone else late.

Equipment and Tools:
Employees are responsible for keeping tools and equipment clean, and for locating all items used after the job each day and returning them to the proper location in the vehicle. Missing items may be charged to employees who last used them.

Vehicles:
Work teams must wash their truck on Friday each week to keep it looking good. If raining, wash the truck the following Monday. Keep all tools and equipment in their proper place in the trucks and in the warehouse.

Safety Meetings

Safety and Employee meetings are held once per month and will include information such as the following page. Each employee must attend, then sign an attendance sheet which is kept in the Safety Coordinator's book. If you miss the meeting for any reason, you must make it up within one week.

Side Jobs:

Employees may not take on side jobs that compete with our business or use our equipment, truck, tools, or ladders for personal use. This is stealing, and we will prosecute to the fullest extend of the law.

Other Jobs:

Employees are not authorized to do other non- related jobs for our customers. Example: one of our customers asks you to mow their lawn. You are not licensed or insured to do this work, and neither are we. You do not have the protection of the company behind you and it would be taking a huge risk. If something happens, the customer may try to sue the corporation. Do not do it.

Products:

Return any remaining product to the warehouse after jobs. Do not throw out anything of use. We keep an inventory of all items and will charge them to you if anything is missing.

Inventory:

Report any items you take out for a job so we can take it out of inventory. We will provide you with an inventory take-out sheet.

Overtime:

Employees may be requested to work overtime during any work week. This is voluntary. Overtime is paid at 1 1/2 times the normal rate of pay.

Job Methods:

Employees must do job tasks as instructed. Do not use your own method unless approved by management in advance.

Lunch:

All employees **must** take a 30-minute to one hour lunch off the clock per 8 hours worked in one day. This is state law. Be sure to put the actual time off for lunch on your time card. If you bring your lunch with you, take 30 minutes. If you go out for lunch, take one hour. If nothing is written on your time card we will assume you took a one-hour lunch.

Commissions:

Sales commissions are paid on certain items to salespersons. If you have sales please fill out a commission sheet weekly and turn in to payroll. Be sure to provide all information about the job. Commissions will be paid AFTER payment in full has been received from the client.

Consequences:
Consequences for not abiding by the above regulations may result in a warning, suspension from work, a fine, or termination. Three warnings will result in immediate termination.

COMP TIME
Employees may take COMP TIME
Instead of or in addition to OVERTIME

COMP TIME is time that you accumulate for sick days or personal days that you may need to take off in the future. Instead of getting time and a half for overtime, you may choose to save that up as Comp time. Then, when you need to use it during slow period you will get paid for your time off.

In other words,
It is an exact TRADE for TIME and MONEY
1 1/2 HOURS OF COMP TIME USED = 1 HOUR OF OVERTIME WORKED

Example: Bob works 4 hours overtime one week. He takes it as Comp time instead of overtime. Then, when he needs time off or if weather prevents work, he gets 6 hours credit and gets paid for it that week.

You may split your choices weekly between overtime and comp time. Put a "C" on your timesheet if you would like comp time, and an "O" for overtime pay. If you do not indicate what you want, we will make the choice for you.

Please read this manual in its entirety, then sign and return this page
to _____

I have read this Employee Manual in its entirety and agree to the terms stated therein.

Signed: _____

Printed name: _____

Date: _____

Employee Non-Compete Contract

(Modify to suit your company)

Note: I highly recommend using this contract in states where it is allowed in order to protect yourself from future competition. It is standard practice to use such a contract in most states but the time may differ.

This agreement is between _____, (employee), hereafter referred to as "the employee." and _____, (employer), hereafter referred to as "the company".

The employee, in exchange for training and employment provided by the company, hereby agrees not to share any company information, including but not limited to policies, procedures, inventions, forms, or methods with any other person or entity. The employee also agrees not to compete in any way with the company, and shall not open a similar business or work for another company in the same or similar business within a 50-mile radius of the home office and/or any offices, warehouses, or stores of the company for a period of at least _____ years after termination of employment.

(For states with unlimited time): This contract shall remain in effect indefinitely unless a written agreement is made by both parties.

(For states with limited time restrictions): This contract shall remain in effect for a period of ten years (or other time period).

I have read and agree to the above terms and conditions:

Signed _____ Date _____
              Employee

Printed name: _____

Are Your Independent Contractors Really Employees?

IMPORTANT!

Many businesses make the mistake of classifying their employees as independent contractors. This can lead to potential problems with the IRS and your Workmen's Comp carrier, which may cause considerable expense for the employer.

To make sure you are classifying workers correctly, here are the guidelines. A worker will likely be considered to be an EMPLOYEE if any of the following apply:

- The worker works on your premises or at your job site at the same time you are there.

- He/she gets instructions from you about when, where, and how work is done, and you set the order of when work is done.

- You have complete control over their work while on the job.

- They work full-time for you or earn 51% or more of their income from you.

- Gets job training from you or is provided by you.

- You pay the worker on a regular (such as weekly or bi-weekly) basis.

- You pay travel expenses.

- You furnish tools and equipment and/or a vehicle.

- The worker does not have their own Workmen's Comp and Liability insurance.

- The worker is considered to be "On Call" with you and is always available for work when you need them.

In addition, your workmen's compensation carrier can charge you for payments made to independents if you don't have a certificate of insurance from them on hand at your audit.

Many states require that the employer carry Worker's Compensation insurance. In some states, it is not required for sole proprietorships where the owner is the only employee. Check with your local state Worker's Compensation Board or CPA for more information.

The Employment and Hiring Process

Illegal Workers:

Your state likely requires compliance with the Federal Basic Pilot Program through which employers can verify the U.S. Citizenship of every employee and applicant. Employers who hire illegal aliens have the opportunity to remedy the illegal hiring or face mandatory suspension of the employer's state and local business licenses. The program makes it illegal for employers to deduct as business expenses any wages paid to an illegal alien. State agencies are required to audit all of the contractors doing business within the state to ensure the contractor's employees are legally eligible to work in the U.S. If the state determines that a current contractor employs any persons who are not eligible to work in the U.S. in violation of federal law, the state may lawfully terminate the contract and suspend or debar the contractor from doing business with the State.

Employment Of Minors:

Check your state laws regarding minors. Most states prohibit the employment of minors under the age of 14. Minors between 14 and 16 years of age may be employed outside school hours and when school is not in session so long as the employment does not involve hazardous work Hazardous work usually includes the operation of any equipment, or moving heavy items, climbing ladders, etc.

A child under 16 cannot be employed or permitted to work in any of the following occupations identified as hazardous: any power driven machinery or the oiling, cleaning, maintenance or washing of machinery; the operation of any motor vehicle; the operation of hoisting machines or cranes, or on or about any manlifts; any place or establishment in which intoxicating alcoholic liquors or beverages are manufactured, bottled, stored or sold for consumption on or off the premises, except in establishments where at least fifty percent of the gross sales consist of goods, merchandise, or commodities other than alcoholic beverages; any other occupation or place of employment dangerous to the life, limb, health or morals of children under the age of sixteen; any street occupation or any activity pursued on any public street or public place (This excludes any public school or church or charitable fund-raising activity, or distribution of literature relating to a registered political candidate).

Additionally, work certificates are required for any minor under age 16 during a regular school term. The employer must keep this certificate on file. States also limit the number of hours a minor may work each day. Start time and ending time are also restricted.

Exception for Parents: Most states allow children 12 and older to work for their parents. Another perk for children working for their parents is that payments for the services of a child under age 18 who works for his or her parent in a trade or business are not subject to social security and Medicare taxes if the trade or business is a sole proprietorship or a partnership in which each partner is a parent of the child. Payments for the services of a child under age 21 who works for his or her parent in a trade or business are not subject to Federal Unemployment Tax Act (FUTA) tax. Payment for the services of a child are subject to income tax withholding, regardless of age.

For more information on taxes, including when a parent works for a child visit https://www.irs.gov/Businesses/Small-Businesses-%26-Self-Employed/Family-Help

The employment application is an important part of the hiring process. The information obtained from this form will allow you to check on the employees past work history, driving record, and do a background check and drug testing if you wish. I would also encourage employers to request a resume' and samples of their work (if applicable to the job).

What you cannot ask
There are several things you absolutely cannot ask an employee, either in writing or verbally, or a lawsuit could result. Among these are:

- The employees marital status
- If they have children
- Their religion
- Their race
- Their credit record
- Sexual orientation
- If they have ever had a job related injury, workmen's comp claim, physical or mental impairment

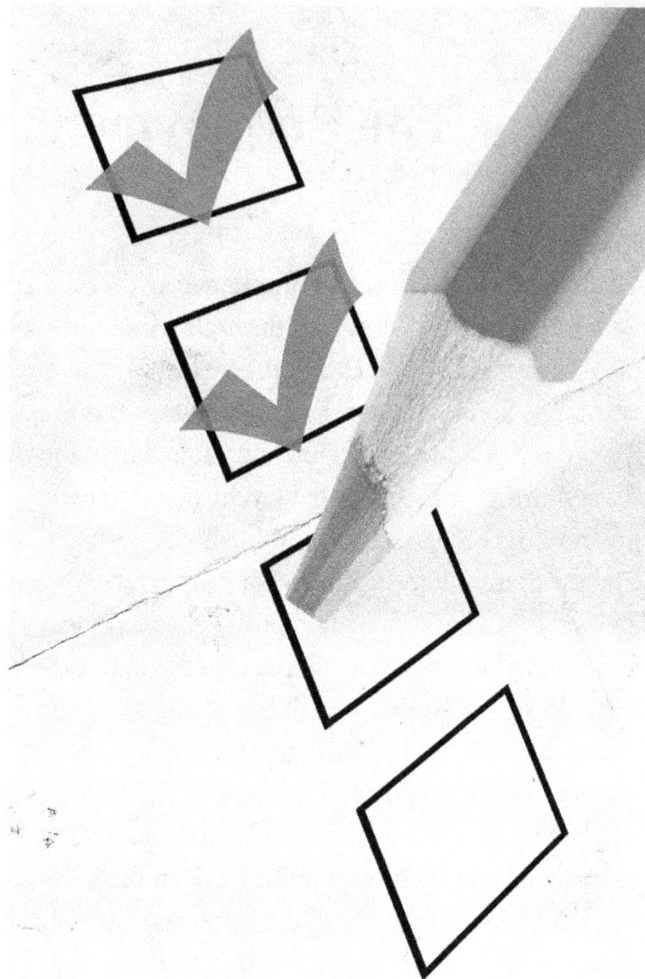

What you may ask about is anything that is related to the job the potential employee is applying for and what their qualifications are for the job.

You may also state that you do random drug testing. This will discourage drug users from applying. Believe, me it happens!

After you have the resume' in hand call each of the previous employers and ask if the person worked for them during the dates indicated, if they were a reliable employee, and if they would rehire them. You may not ask any other questions by law, however, if the employer volunteers further information that is fine.

Another way to check on a potential new hire is to see what they post on social media sites. People's true nature is often revealed on social media such as Facebook.

You may also do a criminal background check by looking up the person's name on CASENET online in most states. I highly recommend doing this because, believe me when I tell you that PEOPLE LIE. I have been burned more than once after I took someone at their word and later found out they had a serious criminal history. The last thing you need is to hire a thief, or pedophile or sexual predator. If you don't want to do this yourself, hire someone who can. Another option for finding public records is peoplesmart.com, which is a paid service online via monthly subscription.

This is a matter of public record, and every case filed in court by the person or against the person is listed. Everyone has a file on CASENET, so don't panic if you see something. Take a look at each one and if you only see cases filed by the applicant, or traffic tickets, etc. don't hold that against them.

On the following page is a sample job application form for you to use and modify as you see fit. I suggest that you check your state laws or consult with an attorney before making your own employment application form.

Employment Application

Today's Date _____

Position applying for: _____

Name:		Drivers License #	
Address:		SSN:	
City, State, Zip			
Daytime phone:		Date of birth:	
Evening phone:		Cell phone:	

Employment History: *(starting with most recent)*

Employer Name:	Location:	Supervisor:	Phone:	Duties:	Dates:

Education: (include certifications)

School Name:	Location:	Course of Study:	Graduation Date

Please list three personal references on the back of this page or on a separate piece of paper. You are welcome to submit a resume" and samples of your work if desired.

Are you able to physically do the job you are applying for? []yes []no For balloon decorators and/or entertainers, are you able to handle heavy helium tanks and hand trucks? []yes []no Are you able to climb ladders and scaffold? []yes []no

_____

May we contact your present employer? []yes []no
What types of tools and equipment do you know how to use?

_____

Do you have reliable transportation to and from work? []yes []no Do you have any vehicular tickets in the last 5 years? []yes []no
All of our employees must be able to be bonded. All potential employees must have drug testing completed prior to employment. All potential employees are given an aptitude test.

Signature: The above statements and information are true and accurate to the best of my knowledge. I give my permission for _____ to request a standard background check from a law enforcement agency and to order drug testing:

Signed _____ Date _____

Job Descriptions

Professional companies have written job descriptions which are given to every employee upon hiring so that there are no questions as to what the employee's responsibilities are. Here are two samples—you will want to make your own descriptions for each position needed at your company.

Job Responsibilities

Sales/Estimator, Job Coordinator

1. Plan job projects, coordinate preparation and set-up, estimate the job costs, order job materials, project plan set up, instruct employees on job plan.
2. Visit the site during the project to check on employees and make sure it is going to plan.
3. Work on the site as necessary.
4. See that the job is completed to our specifications, in a professional manner, and that the area is cleaner than when we arrived.
5. Supervise other employees on the site as needed. Make certain that there is no yelling, laughing loudly, music playing or anything happening that could be annoying to the customers. Make sure that all employees are working at all times and not wasting company time.
6. Check for job materials two weeks in advance of the project to make sure we have items in stock. If anything is needed, place orders.
7. Double check at the time of truck loading to make sure all materials for the job are on the truck. Any unnecessary trips to and from the warehouse for materials that were forgotten will result in a dock in pay for the amount of time needed to travel back and forth, plus gas.
8. Fill out the job completion form and put it with the file. Make sure to list all employees working on the job.

Requirements

Walking, standing, heavy lifting (60lbs), climbing scaffold, climbing ladders, using a lift.

Tools, Equipment and Vehicles Used

Trucks or vans, scaffold, ladders, hand tools, helium tank equipment, sizers, and more.

Skills needed

Math, English, writing, communication, operation of equipment

Job Description:

Finance Manager

1. Enter all checks and deposits in QuickBooks Pro program.
2. Make invoices and statements and send to customers.
3. Do payroll through QuickBooks Pro weekly, give checks to employees.
4. Pay payroll taxes, unemployment taxes, and personal property taxes.
5. Keep a record of all vehicles used by the company, keep licensing up to date on all vehicles.
6. Keep insurance up to date on all vehicles. Check with supervisor for annual review of insurance.
7. Training will be necessary for this position including viewing sales and customer service tapes and DVD's, in –house training with a supervisor, reading of books and software programs. Other training and certifications may be required. Attendance at National and Regional association seminars and conventions may be required, which will mean travel over a period of several days.
8. Provide monthly profit and loss and balance sheet to the President at the first of every month.
9. Pay all bills in a timely manner. Obtain early pay discounts whenever possible.
10. Keep receipts filed in an orderly manner by year.
11. Assist the dispatcher when necessary.
12. Keep a daily backup disk of all transactions.
13. Make a weekly backup disk of data from all computers in the office.
14. Other duties may be required.

Safety meeting and employee meeting attendance is required of all employees.

Job Description:

Secretary/Dispatcher

1. Answer phones, check messages, answer client questions, check calendar, get client information, set appointments for sales people.
2. Keep a calendar for all jobs, inform sales manager of all appointments, inform project coordinator of job dates and times.
3. Keep a database of all past, current, and potential clients.
4. Place orders for materials as directed by the project coordinator.
5. Keep a daily backup disk of all transactions.
6. Make a weekly backup disk of data from all computers in the office.
7. Clean the office weekly.
8. Put sample photo books (or CD's) together for clients.
9. Place ordered items in plastic tubs labeled with the client's name and date of job. Stack tubs in order.
10. Keep website updated.
11. Place notifications or samples of our work on Facebook.
12. Check the mail daily.
13. Take shipments and sign for them.
14. Order/pickup meals for staff in house or on job sites.
15. Other duties may be required.

Safety meeting and employee meeting attendance is required of all employees.

Job Description:

Balloon Decorator

1. Load equipment and supplies into vehicles
2. Keep vehicles clean and orderly
3. Unload equipment and supplies at job sites
4. Inflate balloons with helium or nitrogen
5. Construct balloon designs on site or at the warehouse/office as directed
6. Attend training classes and events
7. Some travel may be required of all employees for jobs or training at conferences and meetings
8. Take safety precautions as directed by the supervisor: secure tanks properly, wear safety glasses as
    needed.
9. Take inventory as directed by the supervisor.
10. May require interaction with clients if the supervisor is not available.
11. Always wear the company uniform directed by the company owner to all job sites.
12. Conduct yourself professionally on every job site and when working with other employees of the
    company.
13. Other job duties may be required.

Job Requirements: Walking, standing, heavy lifting (up to 60lbs), climbing scaffold, climbing ladders, using a lift.

Safety meeting and employee meeting attendance is required of all employees.

Aptitude Tests

I give all of my employees an aptitude test before hiring. This lets us know what the skill level of the potential employee is and where he/she would be best suited to work. Employees who are responsible for figuring quantities of balloons and gasses, or sizing balloons, etc. should know basic math skills including: how to figure volume, measure distance, and measure arches. A mistake by someone who doesn't understand basic math could be a big problem on a job site when you arrive with too little helium, nitrogen, or balloons.

Employees who communicate with customers or write contracts need to have good English and writing skills so your company always appears professional. Don't let anyone write emails, letters, or contracts who doesn't know basic English, including yourself. Take some classes at your local college or online if you need to brush up on these subjects.

There are multiple websites that have services available to employers who wish to tailor their tests for their particular company. The employee may take the test online, or some sites allow the employer to print out the test and grade it themselves.

If you don't want to go that route, visit your local teacher's store and request a math and English test or workbook for grade level nine.

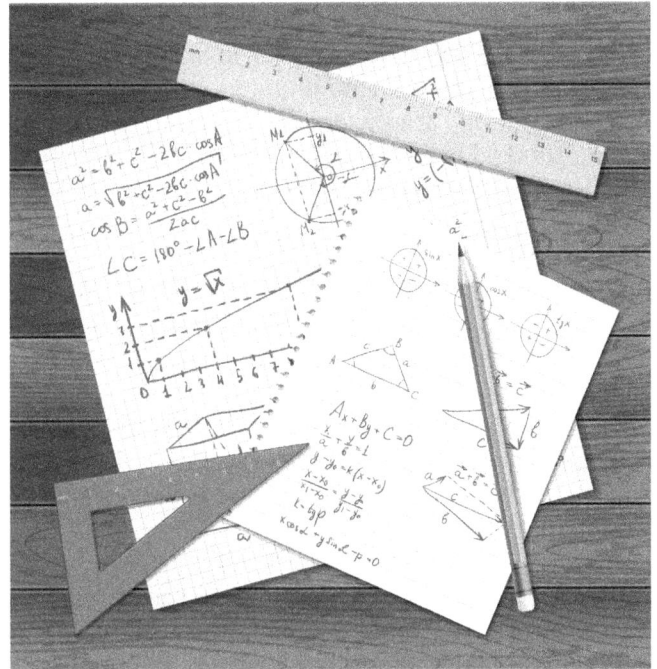

tamiris6 –Fotolia.com

How to Retain Good Employees

Now that you've hired good employees—how to you keep them? That is a problem that employers have always had to deal with—and it is not an easy task. The trick is to maintain your authority while making sure the employee is happy doing their job and is motivated to be at work on time every day.

On the very first day of the job the owner should have a meeting with the new hire, and explain the company structure, who he/she reports to, and what to do in case of a problem. Stress how important it is to the entire company that all employees do the job they are tasked with and to be reliable, otherwise, it could put everyone's jobs at risk. Explain that you are a *TEAM* that is dependent on each individual.

In order to retain good employees keep in mind that there are several things employees look for in a company they work for:

- Benefits
- Clean, healthy environment
- Friendly co-workers and boss
- Appreciation of their work

If you're just starting out you may not be able to provide benefits like health insurance, which is very expensive. You may want to mention that when you can afford health insurance it will be offered, and in the meantime, offer what you can afford such as paid vacations, paid sick leave and holidays, unpaid leave, bonuses, or other items.

Keep your workshop and office clean and neat, even if you need to hire an outside service, or have one of your employees assigned to the task. This makes a more pleasant environment for everyone.

Make sure that co-workers are reminded periodically to treat each other with respect, and that you will not tolerate harassment of any type. Remind employees that if they have a problem with another employee they are to speak with you privately about it and you will take care of the issue.

Do treat all of your employees with respect and be sure to praise them for a job well done at the end of each day. Take them out for lunch or dinner once in a while, put a bonus in with their paycheck, or give them a gift card to a local restaurant or store. These gestures will help to assure that employees know they are appreciated.

The Firing Process

Sometimes employees just don't work out for one reason or another. They may not be up to the task, they could have person problems that interfere with their work, or they just can't learn the skills that they need for the job. Let's face it—some people are just not cut out to tie 700 balloons a day.

Before firing someone, however, I suggest the following process to be fair to the employee and save you money on your unemployment insurance costs.

Step 1: Write out the points that need attention where the employee is concerned and have a private talk with them about their performance. Try to work things out if possible.

Step 2: Hand a warning to the employee and tell them it is going into their file. After three warnings, the employee will be terminated. By having a policy like this, you will have a record regarding the employees work performance or tardiness just in case the employee files for unemployment benefits.

And if that doesn't work:

Step 3: Fire the employee if he/she continues to be a problem. Do this in a professional manner and keep your cool.

Step 4: You will likely receive notice from your state unemployment office that the employee has filed for unemployment benefits. Each state has different rules, but you may be able to dispute the claim if you had good reason for firing and have a record of warnings in their file. A hearing may be called by phone, which is where you'll have the opportunity to explain the reasons why you had to terminate the employee.

Note: If an employee quits, they most likely do not have the right to claim unemployment benefits. For this reason, have a policy stated in your employee manual that indicates that if an employee does not show up for work, you consider that they quit the job.

Employee Safety Manual

Keep this manual in your work vehicle at all times and refer to
It as needed.

Be sure to include the following in your safety manual:

- Contact information for your Safety Coordinator
- Location of your Worker's Comp Urgent Care Facility and list of hospitals in the area you work
- Your entire safety policy and workplace hazards
- Safety procedures and methods
- Safety Rules
- All Material Safety Data Sheets
- A copy of this manual for every truck
- A copy of this manual for your office
- Assign a "Competent Person" for each job site

The following statement must be included in your manual per OSHA:

The personal health and safety of each employee of this company is of primary importance. The prevention of occupational induced injuries and illnesses is of such consequence that it will be given precedence over operating productivity, whenever necessary. To the greatest degree possible, management will provide all mechanical and physical facilities required for personal safety and health in keeping with the highest standards.

We will maintain a safety and health program conforming to the best practices of organizations of this type. To be successful, such a program must embody the proper attitudes toward injury and illness prevention on the part of supervision and employees. It also requires cooperation in all safety and health matters, not only between supervisor and employee, but also between each employee and his or her co-worker. Only through such as a cooperative effort can a safety program in the best interest of all be established and preserved.

Our objective is a safety and health program that will reduce the number of injuries and illnesses to the absolute minimum, not merely in keeping with, but surpassing, the best experience of an operation similar to ours. Our goal is zero accidents and injuries.

Our Safety Coordinator is _____. She/he supervises all safety meetings which are held every _____at _____ a.m. in the office. All employees are required to attend.

The Competent Person is _____. He/she supervises all safety on the job site and is responsible to make sure that all safety policies are adhered to on the job.

Our Safety and Health Program includes:

- Providing mechanical and physical safeguards to the maximum extent possible.

- Conducting a program of safety and health inspections to find and eliminate unsafe working conditions and practices, to control health hazards, and to comply fully with the safety and health standards for every job.

- Training all employees in good safety and health practices.

- Providing necessary personal protective equipment and instructions for its use and care.

- Developing and enforcing safety and health rules and requiring the employees to co-operate with these rules as a condition of employment.

- Investigating thoroughly, every accident to find out what caused it and to correct the problem so that it won't happen again.

- Organizing a Safety Committee that meets regularly under the direction of the Safety Coordinator.

We recognize that the responsibility for safety and health are shared.

_____accepts the responsibility for leadership of the safety and health program, for its effectiveness and improvement, and for providing the safeguards required to ensure safe conditions.

Supervisors are responsible for developing the proper attitude toward safety and health in themselves and in those they supervise, and for ensuring that all operations are performed with the utmost regard for the health and safety of all personnel involved, including themselves.

Employees are responsible for the wholehearted, genuine cooperation with all aspects of the safety and health program, including compliance with all the rules and regulations and for continuously practicing safety while performing their duties. Employees that are not in compliance with all safety rules and regulations will be given a warning. If they are found in violation of the rules again they are subject to suspension or termination.

Employees are required to follow OSHA 29CFR 1910 standards.

Company Safety Rules

1. Absolutely No Smoking
1.) In our vehicles 2.) On the job site while working 3.) In the office
Smoking is allowed outside on your breaks during the day. If you need nicotine more often, we suggest asking your doctor about smoking cessation options or alternatives such as patches or gums. Smoking while working is not permitted by OSHA for your safety. Take a sand bucket and put your cigarette butts in it while on the job DURING BREAKS. NO butts are to be left anywhere!

Note: The company will supply all safety gear.

2. Respirators or masks must be worn while working around any type of dust such as when created by sawing project building materials.

3. Eye Protection must be worn when cutting metal or other materials that could be a hazard, and when inflating 3' balloons and larger. We have safety glasses available in the office and in the trucks.

4. Ear Protection
Employees **must** wear ear protection when working on or near noisy equipment such as inflators. Ear protection should be worn if you cannot hear someone talking to you at arm's length. Permanent hearing loss may occur if ear protection is not worn. You will be provided with your own ear protection.

5. Each employee will be supplied with a tool box to keep their respirator, ear, and eye protection in to protect it from damage. Be sure to keep your gear in good working order and without scratches or cracks. Use the supplied full face respirator guards over the face guard to protect it from scratches and replace them as necessary. When new filters are needed it is your responsibility to notify the safety coordinator to obtain replacements. Put your name on your safety gear box.

Keep all safety equipment including your gear box, safety manual, first aid kit, eye wash kit, and fire extinguisher in a single location on the truck, which is clearly marked and easily accessible. For vans, this should be behind the driver's seat.
3.

Under the Influence
Any employee found to be under the influence of drugs or alcohol while on the job will be immediately terminated. Periodic drug testing may be implemented. Drugs and alcohol can impair your ability to complete a job safely, and you put others at risk if you are under the influence.

Electrical Safety
Per OSHA

- Electrical hazards can cause burns, shocks and electrocution (death).
  Assume that all overhead wires are energized at lethal voltages. Never assume that a wire is safe to touch even if it is down or appears to be insulated.
- Never touch a fallen overhead power line. Call the electric utility company to report fallen electrical lines.
- Stay at least 10 feet (3 meters) away from overhead wires during cleanup and other activities. If working at heights or handling long objects, survey the area before starting work for the presence of overhead wires.
- If an overhead wire falls across your vehicle while you are driving, stay inside the vehicle and continue to drive away from the line. If the engine stalls, do not leave your vehicle. Warn people not to touch the vehicle or the wire. Call or ask someone to call the local electric utility company and emergency services.
- Never operate electrical equipment while you are standing in water.
- Never repair electrical cords or equipment unless qualified and authorized.
- Have a qualified electrician inspect electrical equipment that has gotten wet before energizing it.
- If working in damp locations, inspect electric cords and equipment to ensure that they are in good condition and free of defects, and use a ground-fault circuit interrupter (GFCI).
- A GFCI is REQUIRED for all construction site work whether wet or not.
- If a person is "frozen" to a live electrical contact, shut of the current immediately. If this is not possible, use boards, poles, or sticks madeof wood or othe nonconducting material and push or pull the person away from the contact. Do not touch the person or you will also be electrocuted.
- Serious shock damage may not be visible to the eye so take the person to an emergency room immediately. Internal hemorrhages, destruction of tissues, nerves, and muscles may occur.
- Always touch something metal before filling a vehicle with gasoline to discharge static electricity.

   Always use caution when working near electricity

In case of Job Site Injury that Requires Medical Attention:

1. If life-threatening, call 911 or have someone drive you to the emergency room immediately

2. If not life-threatening treat minor injuries on site or go to this Urgent Care location:

_____

3. Contact the Safety Coordinator or Supervisor immediately

4. You must report all job site injuries to the Safety Coordinator as soon as possible or Worker's Comp may not cover the injury.

Mandatory First Aid and CPR Training

All employees working in the field are required to attend Red Cross First Aid and CPR training every three years. After successful completion of training a card will be issued which should be carried in your wallet. This training can save the life of another employee, or perhaps someday you will need help from another employee. Office staff are not required, but are encouraged to take the training as well.

You will learn how to identify serious life-threatening situations, when to call 911, and how to administer first aid and CPR. This training may come in handy at other times when you are not at work.

Ask the Safety Coordinator when the next training session will be. You may be able to attend local Red Cross sessions, or sessions sponsored by chimney associations.

WARNING: **The practice of intentionally inhaling helium for a voice-altering effect is extremely dangerous and may result in serious injury or death!**

Do NOT breathe helium. Breathing in helium displaces oxygen from the lungs which in turn, deprives vital organs of essential oxygen. This is most acutely seen in the brain which can only manage 5-6 seconds before the person becomes unconscious.
Apart from a high-pitched voice, potential health effects of helium are dizziness, headache and suffocation. Should anyone experience ill effects from inhaling helium, the advice is to get the person to breathe in fresh air immediately.
If symptoms persist, oxygen may need to be administered, so get medical help urgently.

Choking Hazard - Children under 8 years can choke or suffocate on uninflated or broken balloons. Adult supervision required. Keep uninflated balloons from children. Discard broken balloons at once.

Modified-Duty Policy

As required by Worker's Compensation

Our company worker's compensation program has several distinct goals:
1. To provide employees with prompt, high-quality care for their work related injuries.
2. To compensate workers during the time they are disabled and unable to work.
3. To return injured employees to full duty in the work force as soon as possible.
4. To help us achieve these goals, we have instituted a modified-duty policy.

Modified duty is temporary (usually no longer than 45 days). It is a process that provides wages for an injured employee during recovery.

Procedure
If you are injured on the job, the following procedures will be used:

1. See your supervisor. If necessary, you will be sent to our medical provider for treatment.
2. The Accident Reporting and Treatment Form will be filled out; by signing the form promptly, you will ensure that there are no delays in paying indemnity wages, if needed.
3. The medical provider will identify any injury-related restrictions: for example, limits on the amount you can lift or pull, limits on motion, etc.
4. If work is available within the restrictions specified by the doctor, you will be offered an appropriate modified duty position. You physical restrictions will be reviewed weekly (or as required) to ensure progress toward return to full duty.

Ladder Safety Rules

Method #1: OSHA rules are 4:1 ratio:
This means that a 20-ft ladder will need to be 5 feet from the side of the house at the bottom of the ladder.
EXAMPLE: A 40-ft ladder needs to be set up to so it measures 10 feet from the side of the house at the bottom of the ladder.

Method #2: Place a level on a rung of the ladder. If it is level, you have it the right distance from the house. Remember to tie ladders off with a bungee cord. Place the ladder on a clean, flat surface and use levelers as necessary. For decks: Nail a 2 x 4 board onto decks and place the foot of the ladder next to it to keep it from sliding on a slippery surface. Use the standoff instead of leaning the ladder against gutters in order to protect the gutter.

POWER LINES: Do NOT use ladders near power lines where they could fall and touch them. You may DIE if this happens. Electricity can jump several feet from the power line, so you don't need to have contact with it to get shocked. Check trees for hidden power lines. When you set up there should be no power lines within 10 feet of you, a ladder or scaffold. If necessary, call the electric company to install insulation on the lines and return to do the work later, or ideally this will be arranged before arriving on the job site.

Scaffold Procedures:

- Obtain training from the competent person before attempting to build scaffold on your own
- Always use scaffold when doing any work that you cannot reach easily with a ladder on larger jobs. Make sure that you are allowed to use scaffold in the venue since many have rules that only their employees can use this type of equipment. A lift may be required instead.
- It is safest to have two people build scaffold rather than one
- Use all braces and pins when assembling scaffold
- Be sure that safety rails are in place.
- Use approved walk boards only (no plywood)
- Be sure to tie scaffold to the structure
- Don't overload one side—make loads even on scaffold
- No more than two persons on the scaffold at one time

In case of Heart Attack
DO YOUR OWN CPR!

SAVE YOURSELF!

If you think you are having a heart
attack, call 911 and do this:
**Breathe in deeply, and cough hard. Do this every
two seconds until help arrives. Take an aspirin, too,
or put one under your tongue.**

The heart gets compressed and pushes blood through with every
hard cough. Do not try to drive or move because you could pass
out. Just concentrate on breathing an coughing to keep your blood
pumping—and stay alive!

Signs of a heart attack:
Chest pain which may feel like a tight band around the chest, bad
indigestion, heaviness on the chest, heavy pressure; Also rapid
pulse, shortness of breath, sweating, nausea or vomiting, light-
headedness, dizziness, fainting, anxiety, cough. Some "silent" heart
attacks have no symptoms.

Contributing factors:
Male gender, smoking, high blood pressure, over age 65, too much
fat in the diet, high LDL cholesterol, kidney disease, diabetes.

Avoid Heat Exhaustion

Heat exhaustion can be very serious

- On hot days, start jobs early so you can leave the job site earlier to avoid sun exposure.
- Drink plenty of water-about a cup every 15-20 minutes.
- Avoid alcohol or caffeine, which causes the body to lose water and increases the risk of heat illnesses. This means no sodas!
- Wear light, loose fitting breathable clothing, such as cotton.
- Take short breaks in cool, shaded areas to allow your body to cool down.
- **Build scaffold up one extra stage and put tarps on the sun side for shade. This will lower the temperature by 10 degrees! If you are working on the ground, rig up a tarp over your work area or work in the shade.**
- Bring a fan to use on site to circulate air
- Eat salty foods or drink salty beverages if you feel dehydrated.
- Avoid eating large meals before working in a hot environment.

Signs of Heat Exhaustion:

Headaches, dizziness, irritability, confusion, upset stomach, vomiting, fainting, or pale clammy skin. If you experience these symptoms, take a break, get cooled down, and if you don't feel better within a short time get medical attention.

If you AVOID heat stroke, you won't get it!

_____

Safety Meetings

Safety and Employee meetings are held once per month and will include information such as the following page. Each employee must attend, then sign an attendance sheet which is kept in the Safety Coordinator's book. If you miss the meeting for any reason, you must make it up within one week.

Material Safety Data Sheets

MSDS or simply "Data Sheets" are required in every safety manual for every type of chemical or product that you use. This information must be kept on site wherever you use the products. You may download these sheets for free from any manufacturer website. Be sure to download them all, print them out and insert them into this manual.

Follow the manufacturer recommended procedures to avoid damage to your person. This may mean special gloves, use of a respirator, eye protection, etc.

Should an accident happen, such as accidental ingestion, inhalation, or exposure to the skin or eyes, refer to the data sheet to see what procedures to take. This sheet may also be taken to a doctor or hospital if necessary.

You will need Adobe Acrobat Reader software to view these PDF flies. Visit https://get.adobe.com/reader/ to get this free software.

SDS for HiFloat: http://www.balloons.com/docs/HiFloat-SDS.pdf

SDS for Helium: http://www.balloons.com/docs/Helium-MSDS.pdf

SDS for Nitrogen: http://www.airgas.com/msds/001040.pdf

SDS for WD-40: http://www.wd40company.com/files/pdf/msds-wd494716385.pdf

SDS for Windex Glass Cleaner: http://www.local510.org/msds_sheets/Windex_MSDS.pdf

The following pages are an example of an SDS sheet, which can be several pages long.

HIFLOAT   **Safety Data Sheet**

1. Chemical Product and Company Identification

Manufactured By:	HI-FLOAT Company 13025 Middletown Industrial Blvd. Louisville KY 40223 U.S.A. (502) 244-0984
Description:	SUPER HI-FLOAT Balloon Treatment ULTRA HI-FLOAT Balloon Treatment
Product Type:	PVA Based Liquid Plastic
Poison Control	Kentucky Regional Poison Center 1-800-222-1222
Emergency Medical:	502-244-0984

2. Hazards Identification

Hazardous Materials: None

3. Composition / Information on Ingredients

Major Ingredients:	Water Polyvinyl Alcohol Dextrose Monohydrate
CAS No.	25213-24-5 (Polyvinyl Alcohol) 50-99-7 (Dextrose Monohydrate)

4. First Aid

Ingestion: Dilute by drinking large amounts of water.

Page 1 of 5
Revised August 20, 2015

Inhalation:	None.
Skin:	Flush affected areas with water to remove.
Eyes:	Flush with water to remove.

5. Fire Fighting Measures

Flashpoint:	N/A
Autoignition Temp.:	N/A
Flamability Limits in Air	
Upper:	N/A
Lower:	N/A
Fire, Explosion Hazard:	None
Extinguishing Media:	Any

No Special Fire Fighting Instructions.

6. Accidental Release Measures

Wipe, scrape, or soak up in an inert material and put in a container for disposal.

7. Handling and Storage

Handle material in accordance with good industrial hygiene. These practices include avoiding unnecessary exposure and removal of the material from the eyes, skin, and clothing.

Do not freeze.

8. Exposure Controls / Personal Protection

Ventilation:	No special precautions required.

Skin:	Does not present significant skin concern requiring special protection.
Eye:	Avoid unnecessary eye contact. Glasses recommended.
Respirator:	None.

9. Physical and Chemical Properties

Boiling Point, 760mmHg:	212 ^{0}F (100 ^{0}C)
Specific Gravity:	1.06
Vapor Density:	Same as Water
%Volatiles:	70 – 80
pH:	5 – 6
Color:	Clear
Form:	Viscous Liquid
Odor:	No Chemical Odor
Melting Point:	N/A
Vapor Pressure:	Same as Water
Solubility in Water:	Infinite

10. Stability and Reactivity

Stability:	Stable
Incompatibility:	Strong Oxidizing Agents
Decomposition:	None
Polymerization:	Will Not Occur

11. Toxicological Information

Exposure Limits: None Established

Routes of Exposure and Effects:

Inhalation: None
Skin: None

Eye: Non-Irritating / Minimally Irritating

Ingestion: None

Effects of Overexposure:

Acute: None

Chronic: None

12. Ecological Information

Not Determined

13. Disposal Considerations

Waste Disposal: Material is not a hazardous waste as defined in 40 CFR 261, "Identification and Listing of Hazardous Waste". May be disposed of in sanitary landfill licensed to receive non-hazardous waste. Disposal should be in accordance with local, state, and federal regulations.

14. Transportation Information

Shipping Containers: Plastic Bottles

DOT Name/Classification: None

15. Regulatory Information

None

16. Other Information

All information presented herein is given in good faith and is based on sources and tests considered to be reliable but users should not rely upon it absolutely for specific applications. It is the user's full responsibility to accept risk for the safety, toxicity, handling, storage, and use of the product as well as to determine the suitability of the product for a specific purpose. This product is effective if used as instructed. With the exception of this warranty, there are no other warranties, express or implied, including warranties of merchantability or fitness for a particular purpose. HI-FLOAT Co., Inc. cannot be responsible for use of the product after purchase. Purchaser's remedies shall be limited to refund of purchase price and, in no event shall HI-FLOAT be liable for any amount in excess of the original purchase price of the product or for any incidental or consequential damages.

Tools and Equipment for the Balloon Decorator

Here are some of the tools and equipment you will need for a balloon decorating business. These tools will help you and your employees work faster, save labor costs, and assure a professional looking finished product. These items can be obtained from the larger balloon suppliers.

Balloon Sizers

You can make your own sizer out of cardboard, but the sizing process is cumbersome and time consuming with this method. I recommend using a professional sizer instead such as the **Dual Split-Second Sizer**. The digital control panel lets you easily set and adjust the inflation cycle time in tenths of a second. Precisely inflate one single balloon, two identically sized balloons, or two differently sized balloons. Connects to a helium or nitrogen tank, or an air compressor.

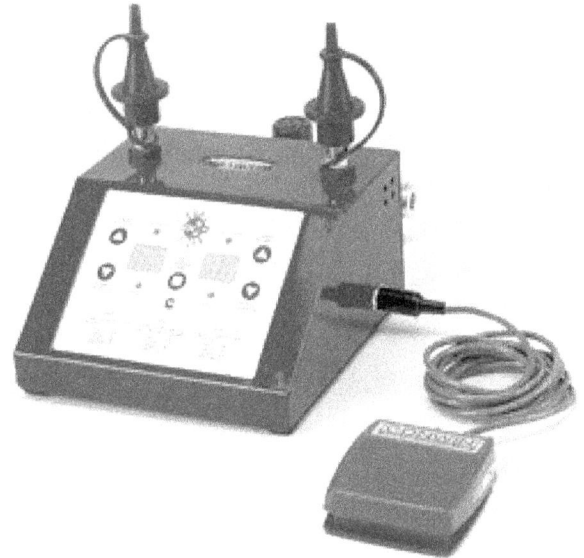

Dual Split-Second Sizer

The Air Force 4 (right) uses room air for inflation. This product allows two to four people to inflate balloons very quickly and is a must-have for large balloon drops or other types of décor that do not require precision sizing. The continual-air blower is designed to maintain a fixed temperature and not overheat on large jobs. New model includes a quieter motor, new friction filling outlets, a foot pedal, a detachable power cord and the air intakes are now located around the base of the unit.

Tank balloon inflators. Whether you are using helium or nitrogen, a good inflator will have three features, a foil balloon attachment, a latex balloon attachment, and a cutter. It's also nice to have a gauge built in so you'll know when the tank is near empty. Some models come with a 10' extension hose.

Hand Truck. A hand truck, specifically designed for helium tanks is necessary to move heavy tanks from your workplace to venues. We leave the tank strapped to the hand truck while working for safety reasons—so the tank does not fall over.

Helium Tank: Optional—own your own tank and save rental fees from your helium/nitrogen supplier.

Master Bow Maker by Qualatex. Makes bows of all sizes quicly and easily.

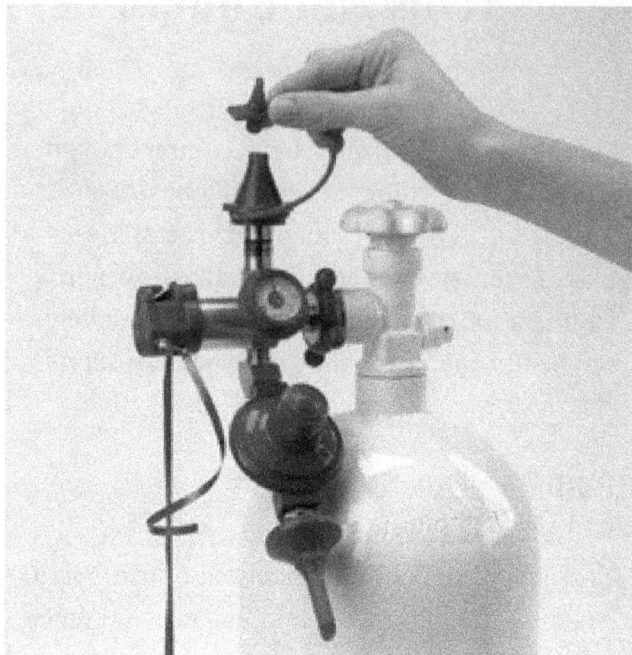

The Precision Plus with Push Valve

Tools and Supplies for the Balloon Entertainer

Whether you call yourself a balloon busker, balloon twister, or balloon entertainer, here are some of the tools and equipment you will need for a balloon entertaining business.

Inflators: All twisters should realize that inflating balloons by mouth, while entertaining, can damage your lungs. Having some type of electric, battery operated, or hand pump on hand is a must for all twisters. Also be sure to have a spare pump on hand just in case something breaks!

Costume: Depending on your style and the type of function, be sure to have more than one costume on hand to choose from. Most entertainers use some type of apron with multiple pockets so they can sort their balloons and have easy access to them. If you can't find something appropriate, make it yourself or hire a seamstress.

Balloons: All types and colors of twistable balloons!

© 3dmavr—fotolia.com

Twist—N-Flate is battery powered and is designed for all types of modeling balloons. Includes a wall charger. The batter will run about 3 hours.

Hand pump

Tools and Supplies for the Balloon Retailer

Here are some of the tools and supplies you will need for a balloon retail business.

Inflators: Tank balloon inflators. Whether you are using helium or nitrogen, a good inflator will have three features, a foil balloon attachment, a latex balloon attachment, and a cutter. It's also nice to have a gauge built in so you'll know when the tank is near empty. Some models come with a 10' extension hose.

Hand Truck: A hand truck, specifically designed for helium tanks is necessary to move heavy tanks around your workplace. We either leave the tank strapped to the hand truck while working for safety reasons—so the tank does not fall over or chain the tank to the wall. Note that this is required by OSHA to assure that the tank will not hurt anyone.

Helium Tank: Optional—own your own tank and save rental fees from your helium/nitrogen supplier.

Display corral: Some type of corral will be needed to contain helium balloons. This is usually connected to the ceiling and allows you to quickly put up foil balloons. It is also useful when inflating a number of balloons for a party, then putting them into a bag all at the same time.

Counter display: For smaller foil balloons. This makes it easy for customers to pick something out to go with a floral bouquet or plant.

Floor Display: For medium to large size foil balloons. This will be needed for any retailer. Displays a lot of balloons in a small amount of space.

Sharp scissors: Keep these on hand for cutting and curing ribbon. Hint: curl ribbon with the back side of the scissors.

Large balloon bags: Needed to keep balloons safely until your customer picks them up. Also prevents balloons from popping during transport and keeps them fresher looking.

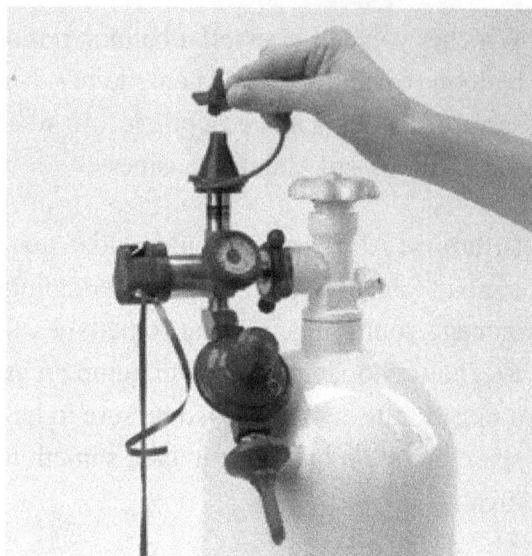

Resources

Balloon Council
This is an organization formed in 1990 made up of retailers, distributors, and manufacturers that are dedicated to educating others about balloons. They offer a certification for retailers. This site has a lot of information about balloons that you should know. check their website at **http:// www.theballooncouncil.org/**
Executive Director
Lorna O'Hara
Princeton House
160 West State Street
Trenton, NJ 08608
Phone(800) 233-8887
Fax (609)989-7491
Email contact@tbc.com

Balloon Artists Forum
on Facebook @balloonartists
Where balloon artists learn and share

Balloon Decorators
Facebook group for photos and discussion about decorating with balloons.

Balloonhq.com
This is a HUGE resource for anyone in the balloon industry. Join to get photos, videos, event calendar, get balloon recipes and add your business to the artist directory, and join the entertainer or decorator forum. www.balloonhq.com

Balloon Professionals Chat List
Hosted by Margie Padgitt. A place to discuss and share techniques and ideas.
https://groups.yahoo.com/neo/groups/ BalloonPros

Balloon Magic Magazine
Quarterly magazine published by Qualatex
www.qualatex.com
Also visit their Facebook page

Balloon Images Magazine
www.thequalatexevent.com

Party & Paper Retailer Magazine
www.partypaper.com

Certified Balloon Artist
Get this designation through Qualatex at www.qualatex.com.

SCORE
Free business advise is available for any small business from SCORE at **www.score.org** Score has information about business plans, workshops, marketing, finances, and technology and is a great resource.

Safety Data Sheets:
You must, by law, include safety data sheets for all materials used in your business in your safety manuals. You can usually obtain these from the manufacturer websites. Here are a few:

SDS for Helium: http://www.balloons.com/docs/ Helium-MSDS.pdf

SDS for Nitrogen: http://www.airgas.com/ msds/001040.pdf

SDS for WD-40: http:// www.wd40company.com/files/pdf/msds-wd494716385.pdf

SDS for Windex Glass Cleaner: http:// www.local510.org/msds_sheets/ Windex_MSDS.pdf

Wholesale Balloon Distributors

These are just a few of the more popular balloon wholesalers in the U.S. An internet search will result in many more wholesale listings, especially in other countries.

Eastern Region:

Balloons 'N More
Silver Spring, MD
800-869-6673
www.balloonsnmore.com

Rainbow Balloons, Inc.
Woburn, MA
800-200-8181
www.rainbowballoons.com

Southern Region:

Balloons Everywhere
Fairhope, AL
800-239-2000
www.balloons.com

burton + BURTON®
Bogart, GA
800-241-2094
www.burtonandburton.com

LaRock's Fun & Magic
Lincolnton, NC
800-473-3425
www.larocksmagic.com

Lauderdale Paper & Balloon Co.
Hollywood, FL
800-940-3577
www.lpballoons.com

Southern Balloon Distributors
Miami, FL
800-777-5544
www.southernballoon.com

Midwest Region:

American Balloon Factory
Overland Park, KS
800-210-7328
www.americanballoonfactory.com

A2Z Balloon Company
Livonia, MI, USA
800-527-5554
www.a2zballoons.com

Brody's 800-4-Balloons
Chicago, IL
800-652-7639 or
800-422-5566
www.brodys8004balloons.com

Balloon World, Inc.
Andover, KS
800-238-5744
www.balloonworldks.com

Mayflower Distributing Company
Minneapolis/St. Paul, MN
800-678-4892
www.mayflowerdistributing.com

Midwest Balloon
Omaha, NE
800-627-2789

The Balloon Room
Vandalia, OH
800-494-0092
www.balloonroomonline.com

Western Region:

Balloons Everywhere
Fresno, CA
800-225-5294
www.balloons.com

Balloon Wholesalers, continued...

Big Fun Balloons, Inc.
Tempe, AZ
800-756-3866
www.bigfunballoons.com

Continental Sales
Sacramento, CA
800-350-4386
www.continentalsales.net

Joker Party Supply
Los Angeles, CA
213-627-1840
www.jokerpartysupply.com

Mayflower West
Cerritos, CA
800-999-4565
www.mayflowerdistributing.com

Loftus International
Salt Lake City, UT
800-453-4879
www.loftus.com

MSR Wholesale Balloons
SeaTac, WA
800-984-1159
www.msrballoons.com

Expos and Conventions

To gain a lot of knowledge in a short period of time, attend one or all of these conventions:

Advanced Balloon Décor Convention
Hosted by Linda Kiss
advancedballoondecorconvention.com

Halloween & Party Expo
http://www.halloweenpartyexpo.com
877-347-EXPO

The Balloon Track FPBA Convention
wwwfpbaconvention.com/balloons

Twist and Shout Balloon Convention
A convention for balloon artists
www.balloonconvnetion.com

World Balloon Convention
Held annually in different locations
www.worldballoonconvention.com

Suggested Books

The DIY Balloon Bible Themes & Dreams: How To Decorate For Galas, Anniversaries, Banquets & Other Themed Events (Volume 4) ,Paperback – December 4, 2017 by Sandi Masori

The DIY Balloon Birthday Bible: How to Decorate for Birthdays, Picnics, Family Parties, and Any Other Fin Event! Paperback by Sandi Masori and Caity Byrne

The Art, Craft and Business of Balloon Decorating ,Paperback – 2010 by Ruth Younger

Kids Show Kids How to Make Balloon Animals,—2009 by Emily Chauffe and Elizabeth Chauffe

Fantasy Balloon Figures and Fairies , Paperback 2000 and 2018 by Margie Padgitt

The Big Book of Balloons: Create Almost Anything for Every Party and Holiday, spiral bound—2000 by Captain Visual

Balloon Sculpting: A Fun and Easy Guide to Making Balloon Animals, Toys, and Games,—2009 by Dr. Dropo

The Event Planner's Essential Guide to Balloons, Paperback—2013 By Sandia Masori and Steve Jones and others

You Can Make $50,000/Year Twisting Balloons, Paperback– 2012 by Dennis Regling

How to Build a Balloon Delivery Business: The Only Book You Need to Launch, Grow & Succeed, Paperback—2015 by T K Johnson

Balloons for Cash: Everything You Need to Learn Balloon Twisting, Start Your Business, and Get high Paying Gigs, Paperback 2013 by Todd Anderson

The Mindful Entrepreneur: How to rapidly grow your business while staying sane, focused, and fulfilled, Paperback—2017 by Joel Gershman and Howard Finger

Guerilla Marketing: Easy and Inespensive Strategies for Making Big Profits from Your Small Business, Paperback—2007 By Jay Conrad Levinson and Jeannie Levinson

Guerrilla Social Media Marketing: 100+ Weapons to Grow Your Online Influence, Attract Customers, and Drive Profits, Paperback 2010 by Jay Levinson

Balloonisms

These are important terms specific to the balloon industry.

Airhead: Someone who works with balloons all day. Not derogatory.

Automatic sizer: A machine that inflates a balloon and sizes it at the same time. Some automatic sizers can inflate two balloons at once. Can be used with helium, nitrogen, or air. A real time-saver!

Ballooney: A person who is in the balloon business and loves their work.

Balloon*atic*: A person who is *obsessed* with the balloon business.

Balloon*attack*: When you have had enough already of balloons!

Balloon Blues Sisters: An obscure group of balloonists who are also pseudo-musicians, and appear at various balloon functions unannounced. Call the police if you see them.

Balloonist: Someone who is a balloon *artist*.

Bow Machine: What most balloon people call the *Master Bow* by Qualatex^{TM}. It allows anyone to make perfect bows from small to giant size every time with up to three types of ribbon at once.

CBA (Certified Balloon Artist^{TM}): This program, a training and testing course for balloon decorators, is offered by the Qualatex^{TM} Balloon Network and can be purchased at most wholesalers who carry Pioneer Balloon products.

Cluster: A group of balloons tied together.

Color wheel: A tool used by designers to help create pleasing combinations of color. Here is a great website where you can purchase a color wheel online: http://www.colorwheelco.com

Complementary colors: Are located opposite each other on the color wheel. Blue, for example, is the complement of orange. Complementary colors enhance each other in decorating schemes.

DriMark pens: Write on foil and latex balloons with these shiny colors—they won't hurt the balloons.

Entertainer: A person who entertains while making objects out of balloons. Requires a LOT of skill!

Eyeball: When you size balloons by looking at them instead of using a template or sizer. *Not a good idea!*

Fantasy balloon flower: An copy of a real flower (or pretend flower) made out of balloons.

Fantasy figure: Created by Margie Padgitt, these are tiny fairies and people made with latex balloons and wire, similar to the wired fantasy flower method.

Fru-Fru: A term used to describe a ruffly ribbon, tuft of tulle, lace, or other element in balloon work that adds a change in texture and highlights the design. *You've got to know this.*

Hi-Float: A must-have. It makes balloons float longer.

Monochromatic: A color scheme that uses shades and tints of the same color. Example: violet, dark purple, burgundy.

Primary Colors: Red, Yellow, and Blue. *You, know, second grade stuff.*

Secondary Colors: Violet, Orange, and Green. *Ok, third grade stuff.*

Shade: Hue mixed with black. *I'll be you knew that.*

Sharpie Pen: The Sharpie brand pen is used for work with latex to add details. It will not harm latex balloons like other types of pens.

Size: Means to make all of the balloons in a design the same size by the use of templates, electric balloon sizers. *A very good idea.*

Squiggle or Squiggly: *The official term for a twisted wire or animal balloon twisted in a swirl.*

Template: A box or set of cardboard balloon sizers.

The Balloon Lady (or The Balloon Guy): Your name when you are on a job.

Twister: *Only NON-Twisters don't know this.* It means someone who twists balloons into funny shapes for a living. Also known as balloon entertainers or buskers.

Wired flower: A fantasy flower made with wire and latex balloons.

Wired ribbon: Ribbon that has wire on one or both edges. It can be bent into different shapes more easily than non-wired ribbon.

Publications and Presentations by Marge Padgitt

Books:
Fantasy Balloon Fairies and People 2003
Balloon Flowers and Figures 2018
The Balloon Professional's Resource Book 2014 (out of print)
The Balloon Business Kit 2011 & 2018
Balloon Décor Idea Book 2018
The Color Therapy wall chart 2009
The Complete Chimney and Fireplace Restoration Manual 2018
The Homeowner's Guide to Chimneys and Fireplaces 2018
Your House is Killing You 2018

Published by Nocturna Press:
The Chimney and Hearth Professional's Resource Book 2013
Haunted Independence (under the name Margie Kay) 2013
Gateway to the Dead (under the name Margie Kay) 2015

Margie is available to teach classes on the following topics:
- Awesome Tiny Balloon Figures
- Write a Killer Professional Contract
- Creative Business Marketing
- How to Write a Great Employee Manual
- Safety on the Job Site and OSHA Regulations
And more

To order any of the above balloon books or to schedule a presentation please contact
Margie's assistant, Tamie Dorsch at 816-461-3665 Or E-mail
tamie_dorsch@yahoo.com

www.balloonedu.com

www.ingramcontent.com/pod-product-compliance
Lightning Source LLC
Chambersburg PA
CBHW051230200326
41519CB00025B/7322